CW00338115

IN FOCUS
WORKBOOK

tarot

A Guide to Understanding Card Meanings and Spreads

REBECCA FALCON

T
A
R
O

Contents

INTRODUCTION 6

CHAPTER 1:
MAJOR ARCANA 12

THE START OF THE JOURNEY 18
THE MIDDLE OF THE JOURNEY 32
THE END OF THE JOURNEY 46

CHAPTER 2:
MINOR ARCANA 60

THE SUITS 64
COURT CARDS 73
ACES TO TENS 86

CHAPTER 3:
TAROT SPREADS 120

GETTING TO KNOW YOUR DECK 126
FORMULATING QUESTIONS 130
YES OR NO QUESTIONS 134
PULL A SINGLE CARD 136
CARD-A-DAY JOURNAL 138
ONE TO THREE 142
PRACTICE A THREE-CARD SPREAD 144
CREATE YOUR OWN THREE-CARD SPREAD 146
FACEUP OR FACEDOWN 148
FIVE-CARD SPREADS 150
NINE-CARD SPREAD 154
PYRAMID SPREAD 156
CELTIC CROSS 158
CONSIDER THE SUITS 160
BUILD YOUR OWN LARGE SPREAD 162

introduction

Tarot can offer us deep insight into ourselves. The cards offer messages and tell stories that ask us to focus on specific areas of our lives. Through this focus, we are able to get a clear vision of where we need to center our attention. The lessons we learn through reading the cards give us the opportunity to find the best version of ourselves. We can see what we need to embrace, what we need to let go of, and how we need to move forward.

WHAT IS

TAROT?

Tarot cards were originally used as playing cards, but have been used for divination as a form of cartomancy since the eighteenth century. While the mystical, fortune-telling aspect of tarot is what most people are familiar with, the cards do not contain magical future knowledge. Rather, they're a tool that can help you recognize your own journey, the patterns you hold onto, and the things you truly need. Modern tarot reading has embraced this side of the practice. There are many traditions and decks available, giving anyone the opportunity to connect with the stories, art, and teachings of whichever option they feel most drawn to.

The level of spirituality that you bring to your practice is a personal choice. Whether you think your drawings are completely random, or you have spiritual guides that you work with, the cards that you pull will give you a chance to explore your innermost self. No matter where you fall on that spectrum of mystical connectedness, you can get accurate and meaningful messages from the cards. The deck is the conduit for teaching you the lesson that you need in the moment.

While there are many spreads that will offer an insight into the past or the future, the practice is very much based in the present. The cards, and our understanding of their messages, provide us with a look at what we are currently holding onto and how those things are influencing our lives. When we ask for information about the past, we get insight into the parts of our past that still influence our lives today. When we look for answers about the future, we are intuiting what our next steps may look like based on how we are currently leading our lives. The magic comes from within you. Your understanding of yourself and your intuition will be enhanced over time as you practice tarot.

MEET THE CARDS

The tarot deck is broken into 22 Major Arcana and 56 Minor Arcana cards. The word "arcana" comes from the Latin word *arcanus*, meaning secret or mystery. As you get to know the cards, you'll unlock their mysteries and learn their secrets. Many of the cards use figures found in familiar stories, myths, and legends to make the symbology and meaning clear and relatable to us.

The Major Arcana takes us on a journey, giving us insight into the big-picture events of our lives, and telling us what's influencing those events. The cards are numbered from I–XXI, with the Fool outside of these numbers representing ourselves as the voyager. The first seven numbered cards represent our guides, showing up to offer their specific wisdom when we need it. The middle seven cards allow us to draw out our own knowledge, encouraging our intuitive selves to recognize what obstacles we may face and what strengths we have to draw on as we journey through our own self-discovery. The final seven cards show us outside influences and universal truths that affect our understanding of the world around us. These cards tell us that our wisdom extends beyond ourselves, and gives us the chance to access the knowledge of the universe.

The Minor Arcana show us more day-to-day parts of our lives, telling us where to focus our attention. The cards are broken up into four suits. These suits are commonly called Pentacles, Cups, Swords, and Wands, but many variations exist. Each of these suits represents an element and an aspect of life. Pentacles represent earth and the physical parts of our lives, usually our health or finances. Cups symbolize water and our emotions. Swords signify air and our thoughts and ideas. Wands are fire and show us passion and energy.

When you start reading spreads, the cards can work together to show us how different aspects of our lives are connected. The combinations of Major and Minor Arcana cards, different suits, and different numbers give us insight into ourselves. For example, Wands and Swords together may tell us that we need to put more energy into our ideas, while Swords and Cups may tell us we need to find balance between our heads and our hearts. The numbers on the cards will show us where in the cycle we are. Aces show the start of a new journey in that part of our life, while tens tell us that we are ending a cycle, having learned what we needed to about that suit in the context of the question asked.

USING THIS BOOK

This book will help you learn the meanings of the cards with or without your own tarot deck, but having a deck on hand will make your learning more complete. Once you begin learning spreads, you'll need a deck to start practicing with. This book is split into three chapters, with exercises that will give you a chance to become familiar with each card of the deck, as well as the practice of pulling cards and reading spreads.

Knowledge of the cards will go beyond simple memorization. The book is broken down so that you can see how different groups of cards work in similar ways, how suits and numbers affect each other, and how you can get information from the symbols on the cards. The exercises in these chapters will give you a chance to interpret the cards and form deeper connections with them, allowing you to hone your instinct. These connections will make readings easier, as the stories the cards tell will come through clearly and intuitively.

The first chapter will bring the Major Arcana to life, allowing you to easily illuminate the cards' messages and see how they play into the larger themes of your questions.

The next chapter, the Minor Arcana, will go over the meanings of the suits and numbers and how to use your knowledge of both to read every card.

Finally, you'll have the chance to see how to use this knowledge in different spreads, and how to create your own spreads so that every reading you do can be tailored to your needs at that moment.

Take your time with this book. If you are new to tarot, tapping into your intuitive energies and knowledge can be overwhelming. Take in this learning at your own speed. You will have the chance to practice writing many questions. As you practice readings, be sure to vary the questions that you ask with each pull. This will allow you to trust the messages you receive. If you keep asking the same questions without taking action in that area of your life, the negativity of your hesitation or insecurity can seep into your reading and make it less effective.

Revisit exercises as often as you need, and allow yourself to add to any answers that you may have written the first time you went through the book. Our understanding of the cards can evolve over time, and every deck can have a personality of its own. As you grow your tarot practice, you'll be amazed at how much new information you get from each card and every spread.

the major arcana

The Major Arcana are 22 cards that epitomize tarot. When we pull these cards, we see the greater aspects of our journeys. Through this chapter, you will gain an understanding of the meanings of each of these cards, and what they mean when they reveal themselves in a spread.

When a reading has mostly Major Arcana cards, we know that we are connecting to the big-picture answers that we are looking for. These cards give us knowledge of our inner truths and pull out the wisdom we have within ourselves. They allow us to take our next steps confidently, knowing that we have the support of our deepest selves and the highest energies of the universe.

The descriptions and order of cards in this chapter are all based on the traditional Rider-Waite deck. While the meanings behind the cards will not generally not change between decks, using a different deck will give you different symbols, and can allow you to see alternate and additional meanings in the cards.

Each card's page has a place for you to list some key words that you associate with the card, as well as symbols on your deck that stand out to you as exemplifying the meaning of the card. If you do not yet have a deck, use the images on each page to write the keywords and symbols that you find essential to the card's meaning. Examine the symbols, colors, numbers, characters, and anything else that stands out to you. Making personal connections with your deck and with each card will make every reading more meaningful to you.

Additional activities with each set of cards will allow you to make connections that will have you easily relating to each card, so that your readings will have a natural flow that makes sense to you. Your interpretation of a card may not perfectly match someone else's, and that's what makes reading tarot such a unique and beautiful art.

0. THE FOOL

We start our tarot journey with the Fool, who represents just that—the beginning of the journey. The only Major Arcana card without a number, the Fool sits separately from the others, representing ourselves as journeyers. The card features a figure on the precipice, which can feel dangerous, but there is no fear. They are ready to take that step regardless of what is to come. The Fool reminds us to remain open to the world's experiences. We cannot see beyond the precipice in the card, so as in life, we can only approach with our eyes forward and take things as they come. We should embrace what life has to offer with the free-spiritedness of the Fool. While the figure represents our journey ahead, we also know that the Fool has a past: they are not a child, and they wear fine clothing and carry their belongings. This is our reminder that even when we are embarking on the new, we have the support of where we have been.

Write the keywords and symbols that you associate with this card, or that give it meaning for you.

KEYWORDS

*
*
*
*
*
*
*
*

SYMBOLS

*
*
*
*
*
*
*
*

DRAW A CARD: THE FOOL

Using your understanding of the card, draw your own version of the Fool—however creativity strikes you—whether through illustration, decorative type, collage, or any other method that inspires you.

THE START OF THE JOURNEY, I–VII:
THE GUIDES

The first seven cards of the Major Arcana will come up to guide you through your query. These cards reveal themselves when you need to harness their specific power to take your most successful next step. While some have similar or overlapping teachings, they are each unique, and offer a view of your situation you may have not been looking at. By accepting their guidance, we are able to embrace our power in a new way.

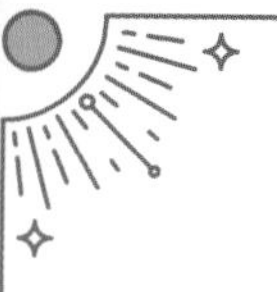
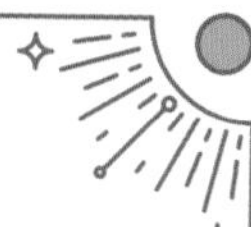

I. THE MAGICIAN

Our first guide, the Magician, teaches us to focus our intent and gives us the beginning of our understanding. On the card we find a wand, sword, cup, and pentacle. The Magician is reflecting on their meanings and asking us to do the same. As he reflects, we see his arms outstretched in each direction. He wants to take in all meanings of the symbols, the spiritual and the earthly, the negative and positive, from above and below. Above his head we find the symbol of infinity. When the Magician is pulled in a reading, we know that we are increasing our skill and our understanding. We are guided to new heights of wisdom and confidence. The Magician helps us to transform ourselves into the next version of ourselves and shows us all the possibilities of that person.

Write the keywords and symbols that you associate with this card, or that give it meaning for you.

KEYWORDS

* ....
* ....
* ....
* ....
* ....
* ....
* ....
* ....
* ....
* ....

SYMBOLS

* ....
* ....
* ....
* ....
* ....
* ....
* ....
* ....
* ....
* ....

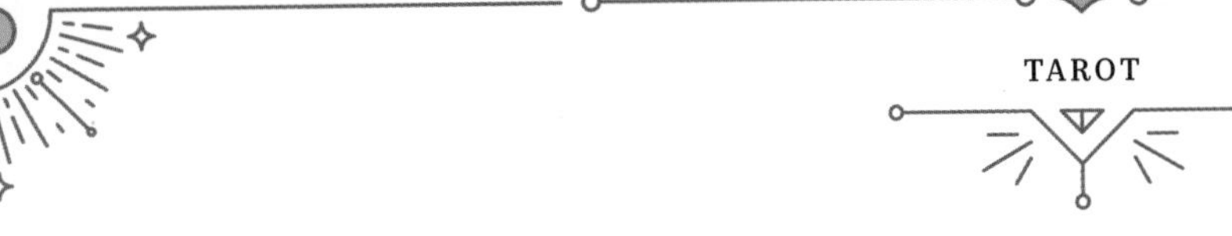

THE SYMBOLS OF THE MAGICIAN

The Magician is the first card where we see the symbols that make up the suits of the deck. Now that you have an understanding of the card's meaning, use the space below to write what connection you see between the Magician and each of the suits. How does his influence play into each of the elements? How does he guide your understanding of Air, Fire, Water, and Earth? For more information on the suits of the deck, see Chapter 2.

THE MAGICIAN & SWORDS/AIR

THE MAGICIAN & WANDS/FIRE

THE MAGICIAN & CUPS/WATER

THE MAGICIAN & PENTACLES/EARTH

II. THE HIGH PRIESTESS

The High Priestess holds the wisdom of the spiritual universe. She has a seat of power in a temple, surrounded by symbols that indicate her wide breadth of knowledge. When we see her emerge in a reading, we should be comforted by her strength and intelligence in spiritual matters, knowing that it is directed through her from higher powers. She knows the mysteries of the world, and while she may not share them directly, she'll offer you guidance. The strong pillars on either side of her place her securely on the Earthly plane, while her headdress and colors are more ethereal, showing us her spiritual connection. She encourages you to trust your intuition. She wants you to embrace it. Through her we realize that there is reason in the randomness of the universe.

Write the keywords and symbols that you associate with this card, or that give it meaning for you.

KEYWORDS

* ____
* ____
* ____
* ____
* ____
* ____
* ____
* ____
* ____

SYMBOLS

* ____
* ____
* ____
* ____
* ____
* ____
* ____
* ____
* ____

III. THE EMPRESS

This picturesque, nurturing Earth mother brings with her all the beauty of nature and the lovingkindness of a supportive maternal figure, whose tenderness gives us security and peace. She is graceful and confident, taking her place in nature, at once a part of it and standing out from it. The Empress shows us how to be fruitful in our endeavors—indicating fertility that can be of the body or the mind. She is a card of abundance and success. Trusting her knowledge and power will bring a bounty. Her scepter, which looks like a celestial body, and her crown of stars show us that she is not only of the land, but also connected to higher wisdom, which allows her to bring blessings to all the living things on Earth. When the Empress is in a spread, we should allow her blessings to give us serenity and peace, and enjoy the abundance she can bring to us.

Write the keywords and symbols that you associate with this card, or that give it meaning for you.

KEYWORDS

*
*
*
*
*
*
*
*
*

SYMBOLS

*
*
*
*
*
*
*
*
*

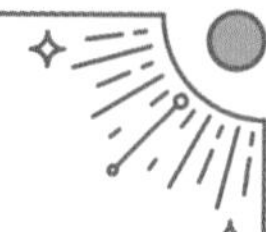

IV. THE EMPEROR

A stable ruler, secure in his crown and throne, the Emperor offers us both his protection and his ambition. As both a guide and a protector, we can take comfort in the security he offers. The Emperor allows us to have confidence in our decisions and our power. He sits upon a throne of stone, giving him a strong foundation for his authority. He is dressed not only in princely robes, but also armor, indicating that he fought to hold this position and does not take it lightly. We imagine he sits before his subjects, an authority on all earthly matters who can offer wisdom to those who seek it. When the Emperor is drawn, we should embrace his power and authority and use that in our decision-making, without forgetting that his power came from conquest. Your authority may not be easily won, but have confidence in it. Be courageous in your ambition, and the Emperor will help you get what it is you seek.

Write the keywords and symbols that you associate with this card, or that give it meaning for you.

KEYWORDS

* ....
* ....
* ....
* ....
* ....
* ....
* ....
* ....

SYMBOLS

* ....
* ....
* ....
* ....
* ....
* ....
* ....
* ....

V. THE HIEROPHANT

The Hierophant comes to us to connect us to the divine without losing our grounded place. He is depicted as a religious figure, with all the appropriate robes and accoutrements. He is seated in a position of power, above two other figures and between pillars. The card has a symmetry to it that gives us a sense of balance and wholeness. The wisdom of the Hierophant is an old wisdom, giving us the knowledge of our place in the world while simultaneously showing us the deeper truths of the universe. It is a card of tradition and legacy. When we pull this card, our awareness is brought to how we can use our past to influence the future. We are asked to take the conventional wisdom of our predecessors and allow it to help move us forward. While the card can be seen as traditional, it is more of a reminder to acknowledge the power in ancient knowledge. The Hierophant gives us a strong foundation to build our future on.

Write the keywords and symbols that you associate with this card, or that give it meaning for you.

KEYWORDS	SYMBOLS
*	*
*	*
*	*
*	*
*	*
*	*
*	*

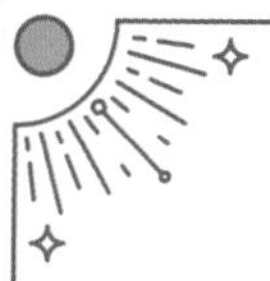
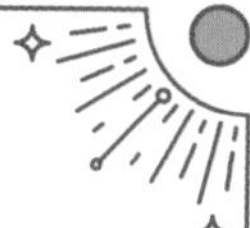

THE HIGH PRIESTESS & THE HIEROPHANT

The High Priestess and the Hierophant are the spiritual leaders who appear in the deck. While similar in their meanings, they have distinct messages and offer different guidance. They both sit in positions of power, between pillars of a temple, connected to the earth and the heavens. They are both crowned and draped in stately robes. The High Priestess brings heavenly knowledge down to Earth, while the Hierophant connects our Earthly beings to the heavens. She has pulled the moon to the earth, where he tries to lift us to the skies.

What draws you to the guidance of the High Priestess?

What draws you to the guidance of the Hierophant?

Does the image or concept of one card resonate more with you than the other?

VI. THE LOVERS

While the card is named for the figures in the foreground, the Lovers are guided by the angel in the center of the card. Like the figures, we are asked to enjoy the light the angel brings, and celebrate beauty, harmony, and fulfillment. We have all elements represented in ways that show how opposing forces can work together. The angel sits atop a cloud—the combination of Air and Water. The Lovers each stand in front a tree: the male figure's tree looks to be ablaze, while the female figure's tree is clearly of earth. The elements work in tandem to create harmony and synchronicity. It is in these connections that we can find beauty, love, and true satisfaction. When this card is pulled, we must take it to be showing us the way to make or appreciate the connections that will allow us to grow together with another person.

Write the keywords and symbols that you associate with this card, or that give it meaning for you.

KEYWORDS	SYMBOLS
*	*
*	*
*	*
*	*
*	*
*	*
*	*

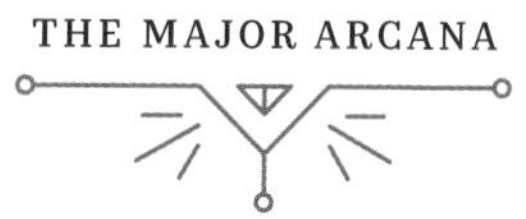

VII. THE CHARIOT

The Chariot is the final of our guiding cards in the first part of the Major Arcana. He is triumphant as he marches forward, reminding us how far we've come in our understanding of the deck and of ourselves. The Chariot asks us to trust our instincts and continue on our paths. His guidance is a clear-minded and straightforward influence. He has mastered the mysteries of the stars and questions of the sphynx. He leaves behind a peaceful place, not to retreat, but to find the next challenge. He does not like stagnation. He would rather seek out a new challenge than stay to rule the land at peace. The Chariot asks us to embrace our power and security and move forward in confidence. We must use our knowledge to push us forward, using everything we learned to find victory in our next endeavors.

Write the keywords and symbols that you associate with this card, or that give it meaning for you.

KEYWORDS

* ______
* ______
* ______
* ______
* ______
* ______
* ______

SYMBOLS

* ______
* ______
* ______
* ______
* ______
* ______
* ______

THE EMPEROR & THE CHARIOT

The Emperor and the Chariot both give us the confidence to triumph. They are secure, ambitious figures with the ability to create success. In both cards we have figures poised in positions of power, symmetrical and sure in their status and their abilities. But their messages are different. The Emperor asks us to stay and rule, where the Chariot urges us to find new challenges.

In your life today, which appeals to you more: the stability of the Emperor, or the adventurous nature of the Chariot? Why do you think this is?

Do these figures remind you of anyone in your personal life? Who, and why?

What images in these cards will remind you of their similarities and of their differences?

THE EMPRESS & THE LOVERS

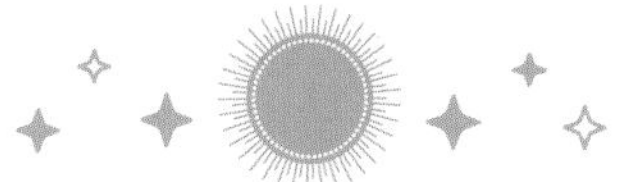

The Empress and the Lovers both show love and beauty in a peaceful way that connects the earth and higher forces. Their differences come in how they express that beauty and how their love is displayed. The Empress is a solitary figure, secure in her own grace and power. The Lovers need the angel to connect them, relying on their surroundings to show them the path toward fulfillment.

Below, write a question you have about love or relationships in your own life.

Look carefully at the Empress card. What guidance do you think she would give you in answer to your question?

Now examine the Lovers card. What guidance would this card give you in answer to your question?

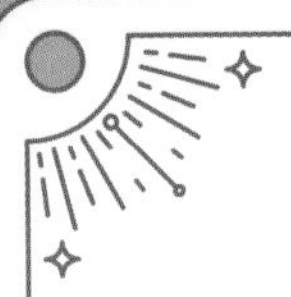

CONNECT THE CARDS

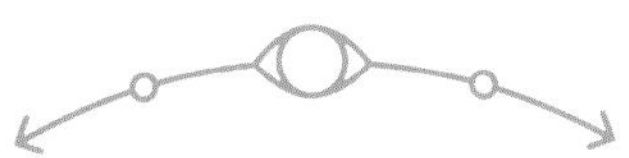

Now that you've become familiar with the cards in the first section of the Major Arcana, this exercise will help you articulate the main themes of each. Connect the cards with the words that you most closely associate with each. Multiple cards can be connected to the same word. There is no answer key—use your understanding of the cards and how you connect with them to guide your choices.

Dreams
Grace
Health
Hope
Skill
Trust
Balance
Beauty
Control
Nature
Structure
Success
Triumph
Wisdom
Abundance
Ambition
Attraction
Compassion

Connection
Harmony
Influence
Innocence
Journeying
Leadership
Mystery
Tradition
Fertility
Inspiration
Intelligence
Intuition
Motivation
Stability
Transformation
Synchronicity
Spirituality

DRAW A CARD: YOUR GUIDE

Pick the card from I–VII that you are most drawn to and draw your own version, choosing images and symbols that resonate with you. If you cannot decide on a card, let the cards decide for you: place the seven cards facedown and pick one.

THE MIDDLE OF THE JOURNEY VIII–XIV:

SELF DISCOVERY & INTUITION

Once we move to the center seven cards of the Major Arcana, we are asked to look within ourselves—to become our own guides. These cards allow us to embrace the power we all have within, encouraging us to see the specific strengths that we hold and become aware of our inner knowledge. These cards tell us to trust our intuition. They show us that if we truly look within ourselves, the answers have always been there. Each card will pull us in a specific direction, to allow us to address a side that we must embrace, making us go deeper within and learn to trust our instincts.

VIII. STRENGTH

The first card in the middle part of our journey, Strength, starts us off by acknowledging that we are filled with resilience and determination. That as we go through this journey of self-discovery, we should find joy in our inner strength. The card shows us that we have the power to overcome and pacify even the mightiest of beasts. When we pull this card in a reading, the beast is usually a figurative one, but all the same, we must take comfort in the knowledge that we can overcome any challenges we face. Like the Magician, the figure in Strength has an infinity-halo, showing us that there is no limit to our inner strength, or our security in that strength. We are energized by this knowledge, ecstatic in our recognition of our abilities.

Note: In some decks, the cards VIII and XI are reversed. If you are not using a Rider-Waite deck, you may find that VIII is the Justice card. The meanings of the cards remain unchanged even though the numbers differ.

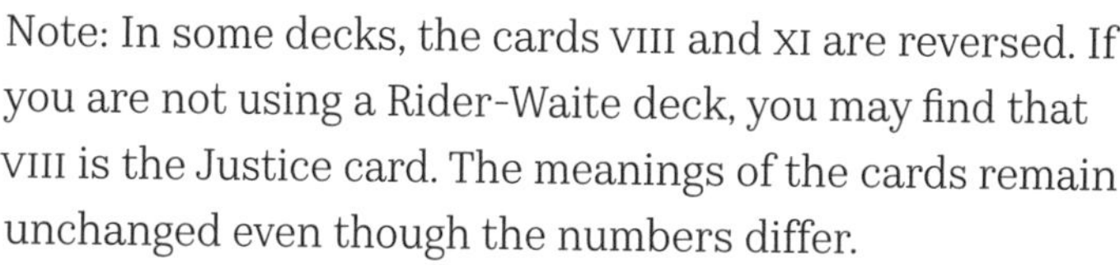

Write the keywords and symbols that you associate with this card, or that give it meaning for you.

KEYWORDS

* ....
* ....
* ....
* ....
* ....
* ....

SYMBOLS

* ....
* ....
* ....
* ....
* ....
* ....

IX. THE HERMIT

The Hermit encourages the growth of our intuition through self-reflection and introspection. The Hermit reminds us that sometimes isolation is not a bad thing, and can help us find our inner light so that we may look ahead with fresh eyes and an understanding that we can trust ourselves. The figure of the Hermit is hooded and his eyes downcast, but he carries the light of a star, showing us that even while deep in thought and not looking toward the future, we can be guided forward by divine inspiration. When we pull the Hermit in a reading, we are being asked to take a step back from our regular routine to focus on ourselves, to meditate on our understandings and acknowledge the truths that we already know.

Write the keywords and symbols that you associate with this card, or that give it meaning for you.

KEYWORDS

* ....
* ....
* ....
* ....
* ....
* ....
* ....
* ....
* ....

SYMBOLS

* ....
* ....
* ....
* ....
* ....
* ....
* ....
* ....
* ....

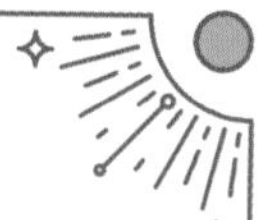

X. WHEEL OF FORTUNE

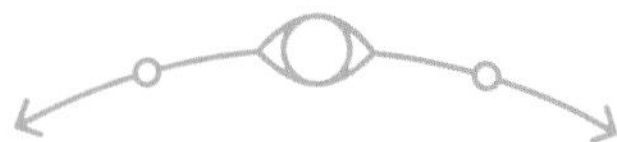

The Wheel of Fortune is in constant motion, granting us new luck when needed. Tarot is cyclical in nature, and the Wheel of Fortune epitomizes the idea that we can use these cycles to make our own luck and change things when they need to be shifted. The corners of the card have zodiac representations of each suit, showing us that our luck can manifest itself across any of the elements. The Wheel of Fortune does not follow the rules of time, telling us that we can, at any moment, have our sadness transformed to joy, losses transformed to gains, and stagnation transformed to movement. The wheel itself holds symbols that give us a connection to divine knowledge, and is reinforced by the figures surrounding the wheel who represent different aspects of that knowledge. When we draw the Wheel of Fortune we can expect a change of fortune, one that we can intuitively trust because it is destined.

Write the keywords and symbols that you associate with this card, or that give it meaning for you.

KEYWORDS

* ....
* ....
* ....
* ....
* ....
* ....
* ....
* ....

SYMBOLS

* ....
* ....
* ....
* ....
* ....
* ....
* ....
* ....

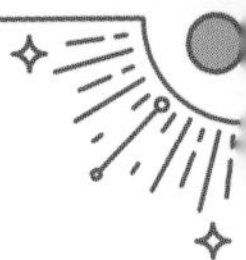

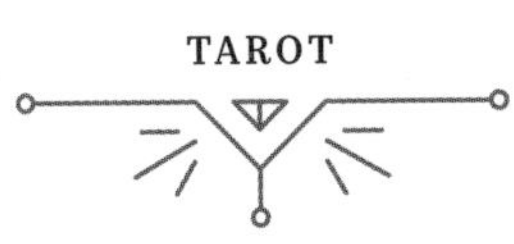

THE SYMBOLS OF THE WHEEL OF FORTUNE

The Wheel of Fortune has four winged symbols of the zodiac, one in each corner of the card. Each symbol represents an element that corresponds to each suit of the Minor Arcana. The bull represents Taurus and Earth, the lion Leo and Fire, the eagle Scorpio and Water, and water-bearer Aquarius represents Air. Now that you have an understanding of the card's meaning, use the space below to write what connection you see between the Wheel of Fortune and each of the suits. How does the wheel's influence play into each of the elements? How does it guide your understanding of Air, Fire, Water, and Earth? For more information on the suits and elements, see Chapter 2.

THE WHEEL OF FORTUNE & SWORDS/AIR

THE WHEEL OF FORTUNE & WANDS/FIRE

THE WHEEL OF FORTUNE & CUPS/WATER

THE WHEEL OF FORTUNE & PENTACLES/EARTH

XI. JUSTICE

Justice sits on a throne with the scales of justice in one hand and a sword in the other, ready to pass judgment. His crown and heavy robes, along with the pillars and deep colors, give us a sense that this card is strong. The card is a very balanced one, and the figure sits with head held high, virtuous, and sure. Justice reminds us that our actions have consequences, and as we go through our journeys, we must remain aware of the influence our actions have on others. Justice is what can keep our world balanced. We must take responsibility for our choices. Even with these messages, Justice is not a negative or troublesome card. It is one we must acknowledge and learn from. Even through the strong symbolism we sense a benevolence. We have time to explore our world and correct any wrongdoings. Justice tells us we can balance our own scales and asks us to reflect on our choices.

Note: In some decks, the cards VIII and XI are reversed. If you are not using a traditional Rider-Waite deck, you may find that XI is the Strength card. The meanings of the cards remain unchanged even though the numbers differ.

Write the keywords and symbols that you associate with this card, or that give it meaning for you.

KEYWORDS

- ....
- ....
- ....
- ....
- ....

SYMBOLS

- ....
- ....
- ....
- ....
- ....

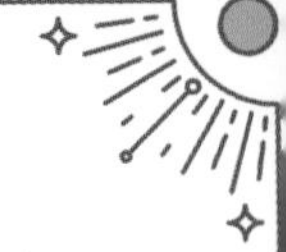

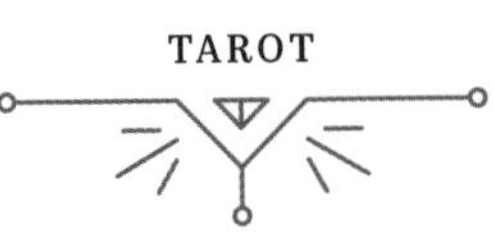

XII. THE HANGED MAN

The Hanged Man offers us a change of perspective. The title of the card is morbid in a way that the card itself is not: the man is not hanged by his neck, but by his ankle. When we pull this card, we are being asked to step outside of our comfort zone to evaluate a situation from a new outlook. The Hanged Man shows us that this is not a comfortable position to be in. It is one that may require a level of self-sacrifice. His halo shows us that this discomfort and sacrifice is for the better. We can learn and draw wisdom from this shift in perspective, growing our intuition and making us more enlightened. We must accept change to be able to move forward in our lives, and the Hanged Man comes out to remind us that standing on the same ground forever will not encourage the change you need to evolve and move forward.

Write the keywords and symbols that you associate with this card, or that give it meaning for you.

KEYWORDS	**SYMBOLS**
*	*
*	*
*	*
*	*
*	*
*	*
*	*
*	*

THE HERMIT & THE HANGED MAN

The Hermit and the Hanged Man both give us a sense of turning inward to face ourselves. Their differences come in how they use their solitude to give us messages about ourselves. The Hermit asks us to look within ourselves for new answers that are inspired by both our introspection and allowing room for spiritual inspiration. The Hanged Man asks us to reevaluate our perspective and let go of beliefs that may be holding us back. Each card is rather sparse, showing only a solitary figure, a little bit of wood, and a divine light. Use your intuition to examine the messages you receive from these cards.

What lessons do you think you could learn in your own life by adopting the introspection and inspiration of the Hermit?

What lessons do you think you could learn by adopting the shift in perspective embodied by the Hanged Man?

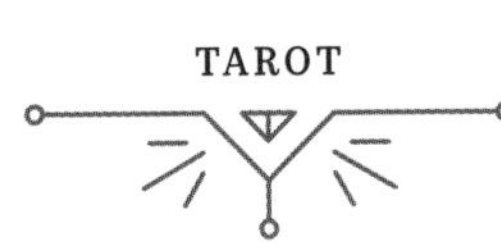

XIII. DEATH

Death comes to us on a white horse, marching amid many of the other figures and symbols we find throughout the tarot deck. We are reminded that throughout life we will face many ends, transformations, and evolutions. Death in a reading rarely indicates literal death. When we draw this card, we are asked to evaluate what cycles are nearing an end for us. Just as the skeletal figure on the horse inhabits so much of the card, change is a huge part of every life. We are asked to look at what we must let go of to move forward. The darkness of the symbology allows us to grieve a loss—change and letting go can be difficult. But we must trust that through this release we are making room to allow new and better things to enter our lives. When we draw Death, we are asked to look at what we know must come to an end and release it.

Write the keywords and symbols that you associate with this card, or that give it meaning for you.

KEYWORDS	SYMBOLS
*	*
*	*
*	*
*	*
*	*
*	*
*	*
*	*
*	*

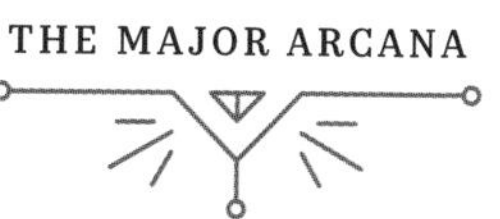

STRENGTH & DEATH

Strength and Death ask us to look to our inner selves in powerful ways that give us the opportunity to make major changes based on what we know in our gut. While their messages both tell us to embrace our power, they come from opposite sides of that coin, with Strength offering us joy in what we have, and Death asking us to let go of what we can no longer use. They both use control of strong animals to show us that we can wield our own control.

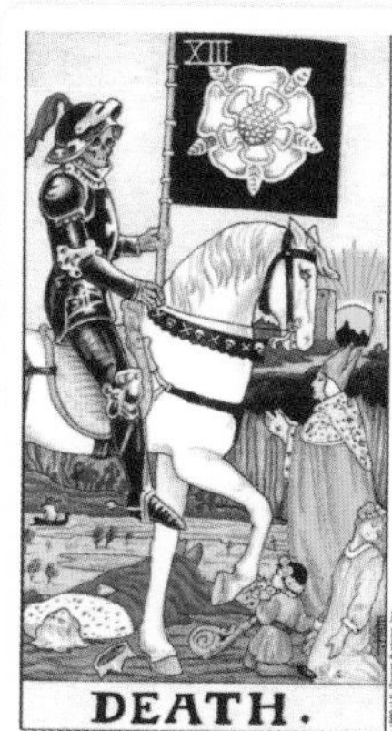

Consider a challenge you're facing in your life and describe it briefly below.

Next, embrace the message of the Strength card, and list the things you have that will help you meet that challenge.

Then, embrace the message of the Death card, and list the things you need to let go of in order to overcome that challenge.

XIV. TEMPERANCE

The final card in the self-discovery part of our journey is Temperance. This beautiful card shows us balance in nature and allows us to tap into the angel's divine beauty and capture that balance. The angel is in complete harmony with their surroundings. We see the rising star reflected perfectly in their halo, shining a light on the divinity of the nature that surrounds us. The angel is mixing a concoction, telling us that we can combine elements to create something new. This is a card of alchemy, reminding us that we each on our own have the power to make something valuable where there was once nothing. Temperance does not waste any resources either—we can be sure that action taken under Temperance is calculated and economical. We know the resources we possess and we can use them wisely.

Write the keywords and symbols that you associate with this card, or that give it meaning for you.

KEYWORDS

* ....
* ....
* ....
* ....
* ....
* ....
* ....
* ....
* ....

SYMBOLS

* ....
* ....
* ....
* ....
* ....
* ....
* ....
* ....
* ....

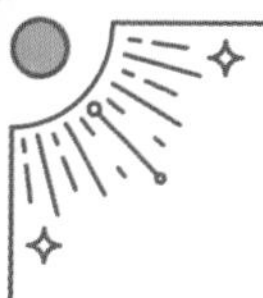
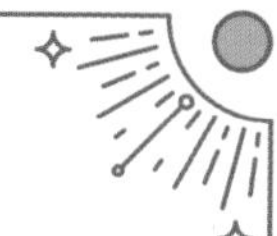

JUSTICE & TEMPERANCE

Justice and Temperance are balanced cards that give us an inner sense of strength, wisdom, and understanding. They both give us the confidence to find balance in our lives and feel secure in our knowledge of the truth and how to use it. Justice shows us balance on a strictly earthly plane, using our intellect and grounding to see the truth, while Temperance asks us to connect to the divine and our emotion for understanding.

Describe a moment in your life when you were able to use your intellect to see the truth of a situation.

Describe another moment when you instead turned to spiritual or emotional guidance to solve a problem.

In general, do you tend to follow one of these paths more than the other? If so, what could you learn by changing your approach?

CONNECT THE CARDS

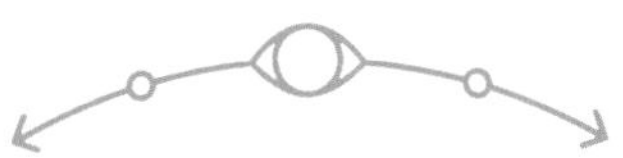

Connect the cards with the words that you most closely associate with each card. Multiple cards can be connected to the same word. There is no answer key—use your understanding of the cards and how you connect with them to guide your choices.

Chance

Change

Grief

Joy

Luck

Balance

Courage

Cycles

Insight

Patience

Purpose

Rebirth

Release

Success

Wisdom

Virtue

Alchemy

Consequence

Destiny

Evolution

Harmony

Perspective

Redemption

Solitude

Sacrifice

Surrender

Transition

Calculation

Consistency

Divinity

Integrity

Introspection

Meditation

Moderation

Determination

DRAW A CARD: SELF DISCOVERY

Pick the card between VIII–XIV that you are most drawn to and draw your own version, choosing images or symbols that resonate with you. If you cannot decide on a card, let the cards decide for you. Place the seven cards facedown and pick one.

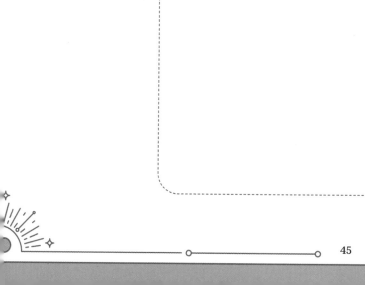

THE END OF THE JOURNEY XV–XXI:

OUTSIDE FORCES & WISDOM

As we reach the end of the journey, we start combining what we learned from our guides, and from our inner selves, to learn larger truths about the universe. When we pull these cards, we know that we must have an awareness not only of ourselves, but of how we influence the people and events around us. These cards represent outside forces that have played a part in bringing us to this point in our journey and are revealing their power to us now.

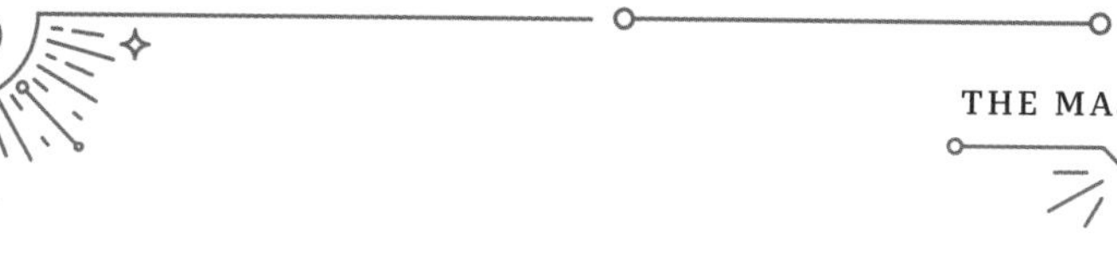
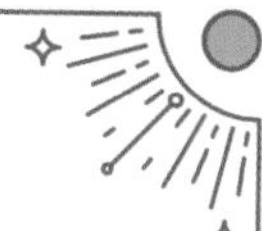

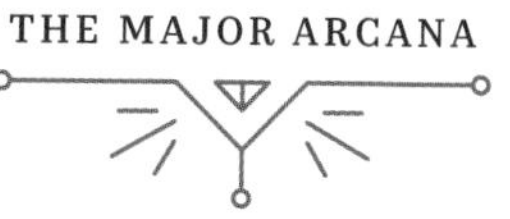

XV. THE DEVIL

The first of these outside forces is the Devil, who comes to us as one of the darker cards in the deck, mirroring the Lovers, but taking on a different power. Here the figures are chained together, attached to the Devil, but we can see they are not held tightly. They may be connected, but they are choosing that connection. The Devil can represent our wants, lust, or greed. He can be seen as creation without regard for outcome. We are indulged by his presence and given permission to seek out that which we may have been keeping under control. When the Devil appears in a spread, we are asked to look at our recklessness. This is not always a negative thing: sometimes that spark of doing without paying attention to the consequences can show us exactly what we need. We should not fear the power of the Devil, but embrace those moments with their potential for growth.

Write the keywords and symbols that you associate with this card, or that give it meaning for you.

KEYWORDS

* ....
* ....
* ....
* ....
* ....
* ....
* ....
* ....

SYMBOLS

* ....
* ....
* ....
* ....
* ....
* ....
* ....
* ....

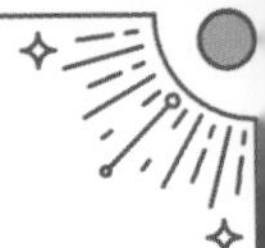

XVI. THE TOWER

The Tower is another powerfully dark card, showing us a destructive scene of a tower struck by lightning and aflame, chaos everywhere. When the Tower appears in a spread, we know that we are in the midst of, or about to go through, a struggle or a trauma—usually in the physical world. While scary, this acknowledgment of this fight gives us the chance to prepare ourselves for drastic and sudden change. Massive upheaval may be coming into our lives, but the Tower prepares us for this—we can feel the ground shaking, and we can see the fire. We also know that like a phoenix that rises from the ashes, we will be able to rebuild on sturdier ground after the destruction. The Tower must be removed to make way for something better.

Write the keywords and symbols that you associate with this card, or that give it meaning for you.

KEYWORDS

SYMBOLS

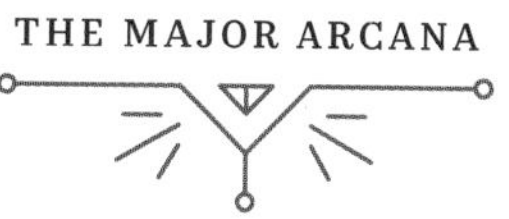

XVII. THE STAR

The Star is a card of hope. Her force of light brings healing from an unexpected place and spreads it to our lives. She has brought us nature and beauty after a difficult time. She is calm, and her insights allow us to learn from her knowledge of how to provide security and optimism. When the Star reveals herself in a reading, we are able to put aside our fears and our insecurities. She allows us to see the brightness in situations and allows us to find comfort in this outside, unanticipated help. Her brightness touches every part of the card and heals us in whatever way we need.

Write the keywords and symbols that you associate with this card, or that give it meaning for you.

KEYWORDS

* ....
* ....
* ....
* ....
* ....
* ....
* ....
* ....
* ....
* ....

SYMBOLS

* ....
* ....
* ....
* ....
* ....
* ....
* ....
* ....
* ....
* ....

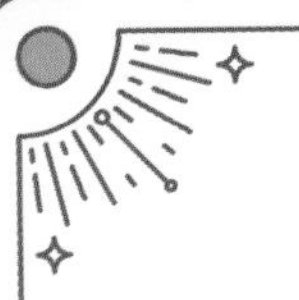
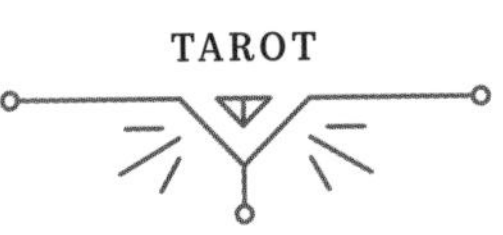

XVIII. THE MOON

In this card, we have the Moon in her fullest position, so bright that the card itself feels more like day than night. This deceptive appearance is our first clue that the Moon is trying to tell us to have a heightened awareness. We are like the wolves on the card, howling at the moon for clarity and understanding. We must be aware that what we are seeing is a reflection: we should put ourselves on alert for deceptions and illusions. The card is dissected by a long road that feels endless. This split is reminding us that there are two sides to everything in life. The halves of the card echo each other, but are distinctly different, showing us how our understandings of something may not be the same as another person's understanding of the same event. When we pull the Moon card, we must be aware of the darker parts of life and figure out where there might be deceit hiding. Allow the moon's light to point out these deceits.

Write the keywords and symbols that you associate with this card, or that give it meaning for you.

KEYWORDS	SYMBOLS
*	* ....
*	* ....
*	* ....
*	* ....
*	* ....
*	* ....
*	* ....
*	* ....

THE TOWER & THE MOON

The Tower and the Moon both show us a darker power that we are asked to face head on. The Tower's force is more severe and chaotic, while the Moon uses illusion to make us question what is happening. Both show us fire coming from the sky and giving power to something we cannot control. With both cards we are asked to look not just at what we see happening in this moment, but at what we must see for our future. The power in these cards comes from the question of how we can move past this moment to build a better future.

What have you learned from experiencing a dramatic rupture in your life, such as that symbolized by the Tower?

What have you learned by working to see beyond deceptions and illusions in your life, such as those depicted in the Moon card?

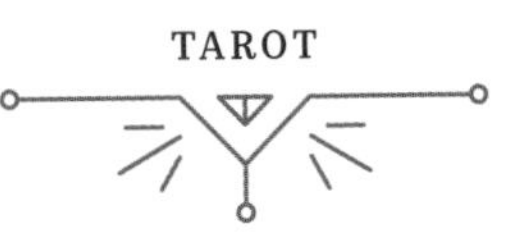

XIX. THE SUN

Much like the actual sun, the Sun card gives a feeling of warmth and optimism. It is a joyful card that presents hope, possibility, and growth. The four flowers can be interpreted to represent the four suits of the Minor Arcana, showing that this card when paired with any suit can increase its power and shed light on what you're being told by the other cards. In the foreground we have a child on a horse carrying a large red standard. Like the flowers, the child is taking in the light and joy from the sun and will grow from it. The white horse they are riding gives strength to a figure who would otherwise feel overexposed or in danger, and allows us to feel secure in this purity and ability to grow. The wall on the card shows us that the Sun is also able to hide things from us. Great light can also give us great shadows—and we need to stay aware of this other side when examining the Sun's position in a reading.

Write the keywords and symbols that you associate with this card, or that give it meaning for you.

KEYWORDS	SYMBOLS
* ______	* ______
* ______	* ______
* ______	* ______
* ______	* ______
* ______	* ______
* ______	* ______
* ______	* ______
* ______	* ______

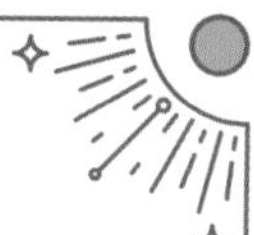

THE STAR & THE SUN

The Star and the Sun both bring their power through light—shining down on us to bring hope and beauty to the world. The Star feels like a more mature card, bringing us hope after difficulty, while the Sun is a younger power, shining its light across any and all corners. The Star leaves no room for shadow, while the Sun can hide its light from us and create difficulties. In both cases, the force is a powerful positive light that gives us the chance to evaluate how we can capture the beauty and hope that surrounds us in nature and throughout our world.

How do these cards affect you in similar ways? In different ways? What are some similarities and differences in their symbols and meanings?

SIMILARITIES

* ....
* ....
* ....
* ....

DIFFERENCES

* ....
* ....
* ....
* ....

XX. JUDGEMENT

As the penultimate card of the Major Arcana, Judgement shows us that we are nearing the end of a cycle. We have so much knowledge and can take decisive action based on that knowledge. We are called to that action. This is the final reckoning, our call to make any final changes before this journey is over. We are getting closure on the subject that we are asking about. We are asked to acknowledge our accomplishments so that we may draw the power of them into our future endeavors. We are renewed and awoken by the trumpet's call to embrace our success and bring it forward with us. When we pull this card, we must hear the trumpet sound and face what we have done to get that resolution and prepare for our next journey.

Write the keywords and symbols that you associate with this card, or that give it meaning for you.

KEYWORDS

* ______
* ______
* ______
* ______
* ______
* ______
* ______
* ______
* ______

SYMBOLS

* ______
* ______
* ______
* ______
* ______
* ______
* ______
* ______
* ______

THE DEVIL & JUDGEMENT

The Devil and Judgement both give power to our choices, our creations, and our abilities. Their differences come in what we've created and how we've found success. The Devil can be the darker side of that creation, while Judgement asks us to be proud of what we've done. Both show us divine figures who look to us for an acknowledgment of our own power, to see how we've been able to grab on to their force and use it for ourselves.

What are some of the darker moments or choices you've made in the life you've created?

What are some of the moments and choices you're most proud of?

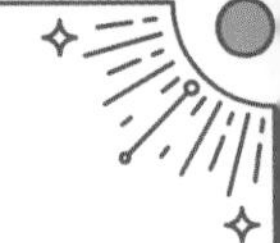

XXI. THE WORLD

The World is the final card of the Major Arcana. It is a card of wisdom, and security in that wisdom. There is a completion to the journey once we get to this card. Our figure is self-assured, dancing in her space, and surrounded by a garland that protects and supports her. We must recognize our own power and the knowledge we have gained and claim our place. We must be unbothered by that which surrounds us because, like her, we are secure in our own power. In each corner of the card, we have a symbol representing the four elements, which she has mastery over. Their presence supports her, but they cannot interfere with her dance or her power. The symbols of infinity holding her garland together show that she will remain protected in this complete circle. We must acknowledge and celebrate our own successes, triumphs, and wisdom.

Write the keywords and symbols that you associate with this card, or that give it meaning for you.

KEYWORDS	SYMBOLS
*	*
*	*
*	*
*	*
*	*
*	*
*	*
*	*
*	*

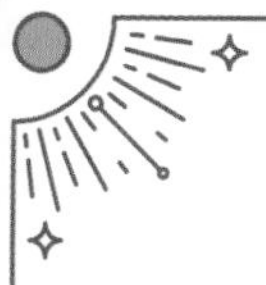

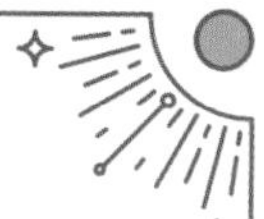

THE SYMBOLS OF THE WORLD

The World, like the Wheel of Fortune, has four symbols of the zodiac: this time they are each in a cloud in each corner of the card. Each symbol represents an element that corresponds to a suit of the Minor Arcana. Again we have the bull representing Taurus and Earth, the lion Leo and Fire, the eagle Scorpio and Water, and water-bearer Aquarius representing Air. Now that you have an understanding of the card's meaning, use the space below to write what connection you see between the World and each of the suits. How does the World's influence play into each of the elements? How does it guide your understanding of Air, Fire, Water, and Earth?

THE WORLD & SWORDS/AIR

THE WORLD & WANDS/FIRE

THE WORLD & CUPS/WATER

THE WORLD & PENTACLES/EARTH

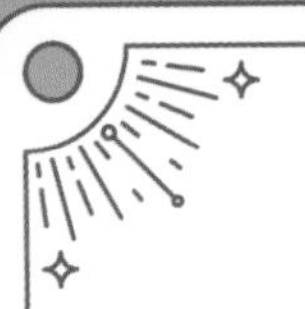

CONNECT THE CARDS

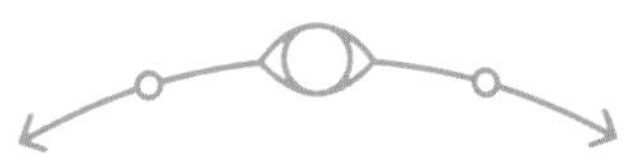

Connect the cards with the words that you most closely associate with each. Multiple cards can be connected to the same word. There is no answer key—use your understanding of the cards and how you connect with them to guide your choices.

Change
Greed
Hope
Joy
Light
Lust
Action
Chaos
Closure
Danger
Darkness
Impulse
Insight
Madness
Rebirth
Shadow
Success
Triumph

Wholeness
Ambition
Completion
Deception
Destruction
Fulfillment
Illusion
Trickery
Accomplishment
Awakening
Celebration
Inspiration
Perseverance
Resolution
Satisfaction
Serenity
Insecurity

DRAW A CARD: OUTSIDE FORCES

Pick the card between XV–XXI that you are most drawn to and draw your own version, including images and symbols that resonate with you. If you cannot decide on a card, let the cards decide for you. Place the seven cards facedown and pick one.

the minor arcana

While the Major Arcana allowed us to focus on big-picture aspects of our lives, the Minor Arcana gives us the chance to focus in on the details and gain clarity on our day-to-day to see how we should be moving forward.

The Minor Arcana are comprised of four suits, generally called Pentacles, Cups, Swords, and Wands. Each suit represents an element as well as a particular aspect of life. There are fourteen cards in each suit: four court cards and numbers from ace to ten.

In this chapter, we will explore how each suit expresses itself as it occurs in each number, and how using the relationships between the numbers, suits, and combinations of cards can offer tremendous insight into the situations that arise in daily life.

The Minor Arcana also show us how the elements relate to each other, and learning how they work together or in opposition to each other is just as important as learning the cards individually. Just as Water and Fire oppose each other in nature, Wands and Cups can fight for your attention in a reading. Just as Water feeds Earth, Cups and Pentacles can work together to connect your physical self with your emotional well-being. Seeing these relationships between the elements and how they correspond to specific facets of your life will help deepen your understanding of any readings that you do.

As in the Major Arcana chapter, each card's entry has a place for you to list some keywords that you associate with the card, as well as symbols on your deck that stand out to you as exemplifying the meaning of the card. If you do not yet have a deck, use the images on each page to write the keywords and symbols that will help you remember the card's meaning. Making personal connections with your deck and with each card will make every reading more meaningful to you.

The activities in this chapter will assist you in seeing how the elements and numerology work together to paint a clear picture with the cards. Once you make these connections, you will have the chance to make the deck talk to you in a clear way.

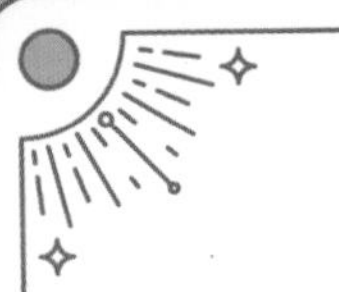

PENTACLES

The suit of Pentacles, sometimes referred to as Coins or Disks, represents the element of Earth and relates to matters on the physical plane. When we pull these cards, we are being asked to look at aspects of our life relating to the material world. This can relate to our health and bodies, or to our possessions, living situations, career, or finances. When a spread reveals a majority of Pentacles, we are being asked to pay special attention to these physical aspects of our lives and to place our focus on grounding ourselves. Pentacles asks us to be in tune with the world around us, and our physical place in it. The same way Earth is the most stable and least moveable of the elements, Pentacles is the most resilient and reliable of the suits. This can work in your favor when seeking security and against you when you're trying to make life changes.

With this understanding of Pentacles, list some positive and negative characteristics that you would associate with this suit and the element of Earth.

POSITIVE

* ____________________
* ____________________
* ____________________
* ____________________
* ____________________
* ____________________
* ____________________
* ____________________

NEGATIVE

* ____________________
* ____________________
* ____________________
* ____________________
* ____________________
* ____________________
* ____________________
* ____________________

DRAW YOUR SYMBOL: PENTACLES

Think about a symbol that represents Earth to you. Use the space below to draw what you would use as a symbol of Earth for the suit of Pentacles if you were designing your own deck. Be creative! There's no limit here: your suit can be as close to or far from the traditional idea of the suit as you'd like. Does the idea of a Pentacle, Coin, or Disk resonate strongly with you, or is there another image that comes to mind?

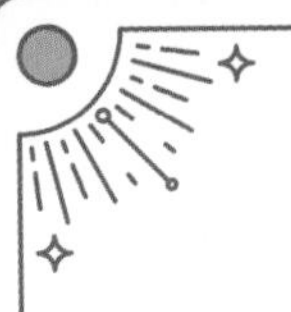

CUPS

The suit of Cups, also known as Chalices, Goblets, or Vessels, represents the element of Water, and relates to our emotions. When Cups appear in our cards, we should bring our awareness to our hearts and feelings. Checking in with our emotions can guide our relationships, our intuition, our reactions, and our creativity. Water is the most versatile of elements, which allows Cups to occur in readings in infinite ways. We must acknowledge the times when our emotions are overpowering, like a tsunami, and when they are calm and steady as a river. Throughout the deck, we'll see that some Cups are pictured full or overflowing, while others appear empty. The variety we experience will allow us to explore our emotional selves and understand on a deeper level what the focus of our heart energy should be.

With this understanding of Cups, list some positive and negative characteristics that you would associate with this suit and the element of Water.

POSITIVE

* ____________________
* ____________________
* ____________________
* ____________________
* ____________________
* ____________________
* ____________________
* ____________________

NEGATIVE

* ____________________
* ____________________
* ____________________
* ____________________
* ____________________
* ____________________
* ____________________
* ____________________

DRAW YOUR SYMBOL: CUPS

Think about a symbol that represents Water to you. Use the space below to draw what you would use as a symbol of Water for the suit of Cups if you were designing your own deck. Be creative! There's no limit here: your suit can be as close to or far from the traditional idea of the suit as you'd like. Does the idea of a Cup or Vessel resonate strongly with you, or is there another image that comes to mind when you consider emotions and water?

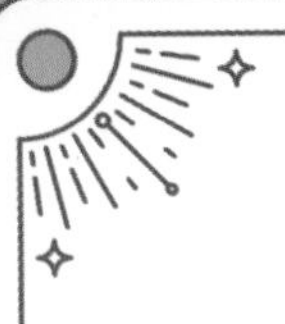

SWORDS

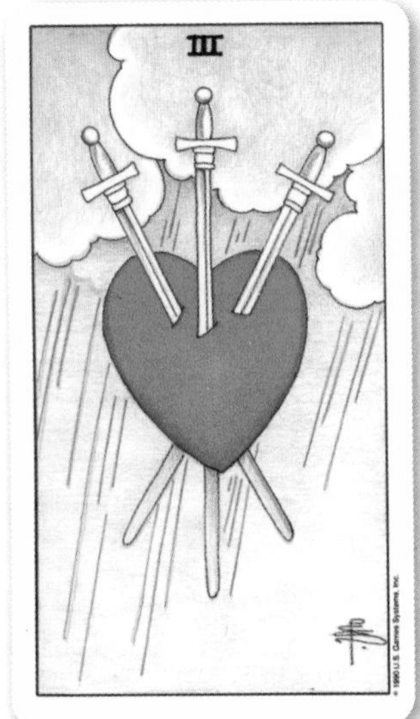

The suit of Swords, occasionally known as Blades, represents the element of Air, and relates to our intellect, ideas, and logic. Swords can bring clarity to any situation, cutting through interference and blowing away what's unimportant. Just as a sword can cut through you, and a gust of wind can blow you over, too much of this element can at times be overwhelming and lacking in the understanding and compassion that certain situations require. At times, this can even cross over into cruelty. When we pull mostly Swords during a reading, we have to acknowledge both sides of the blade. We must ask ourselves if we are seeing things clearly or if we are too stuck in our heads about a matter to get a full understanding of what is happening.

With this understanding of Swords, list some positive and negative characteristics that you would associate with this suit and the element of Air.

POSITIVE	**NEGATIVE**
* ______	* ______
* ______	* ______
* ______	* ______
* ______	* ______
* ______	* ______
* ______	* ______
* ______	* ______
* ______	* ______

DRAW YOUR SYMBOL: SWORDS

Think about a symbol that represents Air to you. Use the space below to draw what you would use as a symbol of Air for the suit of Swords if you were designing your own deck. Be creative! There's no limit here: your suit can be as close to or far from the traditional idea of the suit as you'd like. Does the idea of a Sword resonate strongly with you, or is there another image that comes to mind when you consider logic and air?

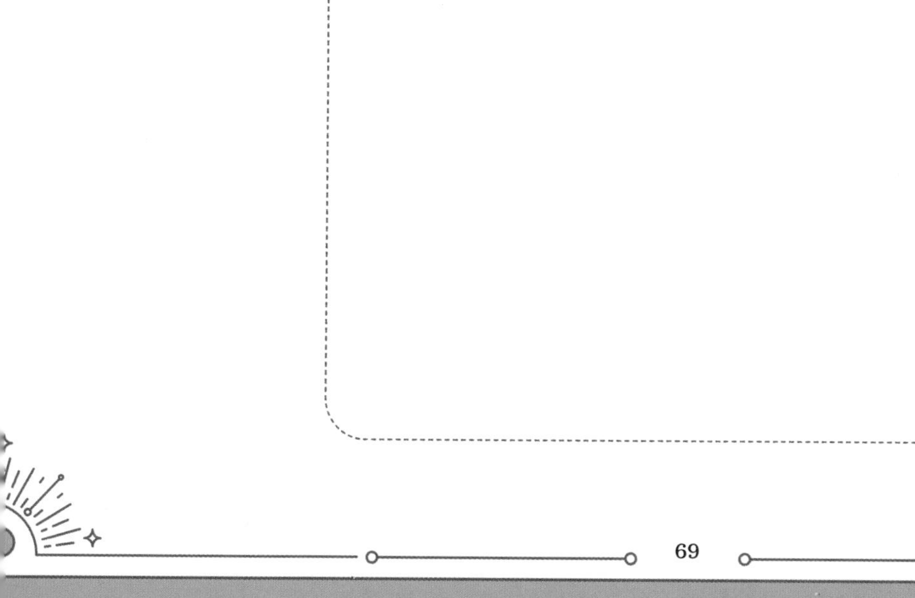

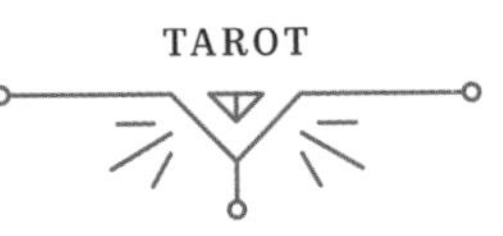

WANDS

The suit of Wands, sometimes referred to as Rods, Scepters, or Staffs, represents the element of Fire, and can symbolize great energies. The energy of this suit can emerge as ambition, creativity, willpower, and potential. Wands, like fire, can be incredibly volatile. These cards can easily go from a power that helps you learn and grow to a destructive force. When we see many Wands occurring in a reading, we can see that we have energy and power pushing us toward movement and the next steps in our journey. While this power can be inspiring and exciting, we must try to ground it to avoid its potentially devastating nature. Learning to see and focus the energy of Fire when it appears in the cards can help bring about the necessary changes that you may be facing.

With this understanding of Wands, list some positive and negative characteristics that you would associate with this suit and the element of Fire.

POSITIVE

* ____
* ____
* ____
* ____
* ____
* ____
* ____
* ____

NEGATIVE

* ____
* ____
* ____
* ____
* ____
* ____
* ____
* ____

DRAW YOUR SYMBOL: WANDS

Think about a symbol that represents Fire to you. Use the space below to draw what you would use as a symbol of Fire for the suit of Wands if you were designing your own deck. Be creative! There's no limit here: your suit can be as close to or far from the traditional idea of the suit as you'd like. Does the idea of a Wand resonate strongly with you, or is there another image that comes to mind when you consider energy and fire?

CONNECTING THE SUITS

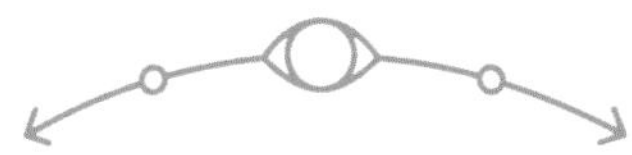

How do you see the connections between the suits? Draw a solid line between suits that you see working well together, and broken lines between suits that oppose each other. If you feel two suits are neutral, do not draw any line between them.

COURT CARDS

Court cards, usually represented by Pages, Knights, Queens, and Kings, can be interpreted in many different ways. When we see court cards appearing in our spreads, we must rely on our intuition to see what they may be trying to indicate to us. In some instances, the card may represent ourselves, or another person in the situation we are asking about who shares the traits of the card. Sometimes they indicate upcoming social events and what part of your personality may come into play in that setting. Like the suits, each court card is also associated with an element. We look at these cards as bringing the element of their rank to the element of their suit, so these cards can show us how to find balance among elements that otherwise might have difficulty sitting together, or give us additional strength in elements that enhance each other.

PAGES

Pages are the young, immature, and naïve members of the court. Their element is Earth, and they are explorers or seekers. They can represent the beginning of a journey, and are excited by discovery and learning. Their connection to the Earth allows for some security when pursuing something new. When multiple Pages come up in a reading, we can expect to feel the urge to explore and should follow that urge.

PAGE OF PENTACLES

The Page of Pentacles represents action. They are diligent and strong, capable of manifesting anything. Here the security of Earth comes both from the Page and the suit of Pentacles. This solid grounding allows us to explore without fear. If you are exploring a new prospect or a goal, start that work and bring your dreams to life.

KEYWORDS	SYMBOLS
*	*
*	*
*	*

PAGE OF CUPS

The Page of Cups combines Earth and Water, giving us a secure space to explore new emotions, relationships, and creative outlets. They can come across as a bit of a romantic, or as an idealist, their youth allowing them to show pure excitement over the possibilities of life and love. This openness allows for creativity to flow. Their grounding allows them to take emotional risks, and we should be inspired by their free openheartedness.

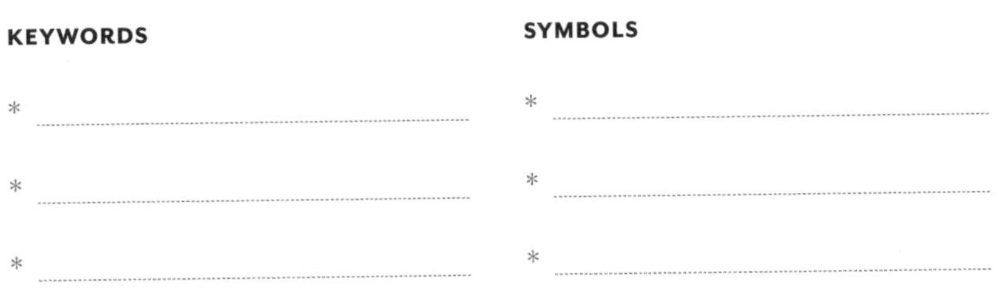

KEYWORDS	SYMBOLS
*	*
*	*
*	*

PAGE OF SWORDS

The Page of Swords is full of energy and ideas. Through this card we are given a solid footing to start on a new project. Here, the combination of Earth and Air inspires new ideas and encourages openness and communication. When we see the Page of Swords, we know that we are ready to get the ball rolling, unafraid of obstacles. This is an optimistic card, full of charm and wit, allowing us to build excitement over the possibilities of what we can bring into the world.

KEYWORDS	SYMBOLS
*	*
*	*
*	*

PAGE OF WANDS

The Page of Wands is the most free-spirited of the court cards. Driven by Fire and secured by Earth, they have the freedom to follow any path that looks exciting in the moment. They have an enthusiasm for life that cannot be matched. The Page of Wands can be reckless, but it is through this recklessness that the spark of creation can be inspired. When we pull the Page of Wands, we might feel as though we are on a precipice, ready to take a next step toward something new and exciting.

KEYWORDS	SYMBOLS
*	*
*	*
*	*

KNIGHTS

Knights are the action cards of the court. Their element is Fire, and they use the energy of that fire to move forward. They are prepared for battle, seated ahorse and helmeted, ready for anything. As we move from Page to Knight, we become more reactive and ready to use our power. Just as Fire can be a force for good or one for destruction, Knights can present us with opportunities for growth but can become extreme. When multiple Knights are pulled in a reading, we will feel especially passionate and drawn to action.

KNIGHT OF PENTACLES

The Knight of Pentacles is the most practical of the Knights, grounded by the Earth of his suit. He is reliable, steadfast, and passionate, expecting success. His persistence leaves no room for doubts and encourages us to achieve our aims. When we pull this card, we are reminded of our own hard work. When we put in the effort, this knight assures us that we will succeed.

KEYWORDS	SYMBOLS
* ______	* ______
* ______	* ______
* ______	* ______

KNIGHT OF CUPS

The Knight of Cups combines the opposing elements of Fire and Water, giving us a charming figure propelled by passion. He is enthusiastic, leading with his heart and taking action in emotional matters without thought. Very much a warm, attractive romantic, this card shows us how we can embrace the loving and passionate sides of ourselves. The combined power of his intuition and charisma offers a deep connection. When we pull the Knight of Cups, we are shown the possibilities of our emotional world when we allow the heat of Fire to lead us.

KEYWORDS	SYMBOLS
* ______	* ______
* ______	* ______
* ______	* ______

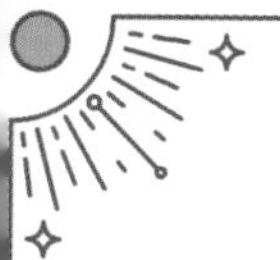

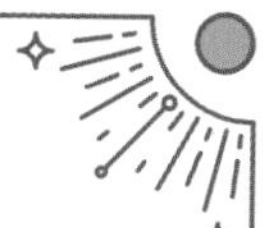

KNIGHT OF SWORDS

The Knight of Swords is decisive in his actions. The confidence he has in his ideas allows him to react swiftly to anything that comes into his path. The clarity of Air joins the force of Fire, displaying bravery and resolve. He is happy to charge into battle and will stay in it for the fight. He might act on impulse, but once he takes that initial step, there is nothing that can get in his way. When we pull the Knight of Swords, we are encouraged to move forward in our ideas, not letting obstacles stop us.

KEYWORDS	SYMBOLS
*	*
*	*
*	*

KNIGHT OF WANDS

The Knight of Wands is all power and energy, taking action as soon as the impulse calls him, often without thought. His rash nature and great passion come across with a level of confidence that can be hard to resist. He moves with so much force that he will not be swayed from his course, even if that course is not the correct one. When we pull the Knight of Wands, we should be encouraged to follow our creative spark, while reminding ourselves to be aware of how we exert the energy we have.

KEYWORDS	SYMBOLS
*	*
*	*
*	*

QUEENS

Queens are the nurturers of the court, providing calming, encouraging, and knowledgeable support. Their element is Water, and they are similarly complex. They have a deep understanding of their element and quickly pick up on details and secrets. When Queens are drawn, we know we have the chance to lean into their experience and follow their guidance. Queens give us the knowledge to make choices and exert ourselves from a steady and powerful place.

QUEEN OF PENTACLES

The Queen of Pentacles exudes warmth and stability. Her outdoor throne, surrounded by vibrant plant life, shows us her nurturing power. Her combination of Earth and Water is life-giving, so anything she touches can bloom. Her presence in a reading can show us how to combine our material and emotional worlds.

KEYWORDS	SYMBOLS
*	* ....
*	* ....
*	* ....

QUEEN OF CUPS

The Queen of Cups has more emotional depth than any other card, but is secure in her emotions. From her, we can learn to master our emotions, embracing our deepest feelings as powerful, rather than being overwhelmed by them. The idea of still waters running deep comes to life with her. This depth allows her to remain mysterious, but her loving nature tells us there's nothing to fear. When the Queen of Cups comes up in a reading, her warmth and compassion allow us to feel safe in her embrace and trust what comes to us under her protection.

KEYWORDS	SYMBOLS
*	* ....
*	* ....
*	* ....

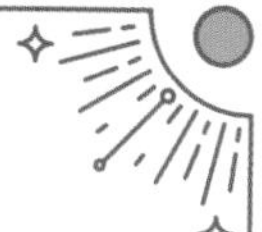

QUEEN OF SWORDS

The Queen of Swords is the most perceptive card of the deck, knowing the truth in a matter before all others. Her combination of Water and Air means her sharp intellect is matched only by deep understanding, making her reading of any situation accurate and quick. She can come across as calculating at times, but that's only because she's figured out the conclusion and the next move before others begin to understand the problem. Her strong heart-mind connection means her council is wise, and her intuition unmatched. When we pull the Queen of Swords, we know that we should trust our observations and intuition.

KEYWORDS

* ……………………
* ……………………
* ……………………

SYMBOLS

* ……………………
* ……………………
* ……………………

QUEEN OF WANDS

The Queen of Wands channels the power of Fire through the nurturing influence of Water, creating a passionate figure who is capable of attracting anyone and anything to her warmth. She has the strength to face any challenge independently, as a commanding and confident presence in any situation. When we see the Queen of Wands in a reading, we should embrace our talents and our drive, and be self-assured in our actions as we move forward in our journeys.

KEYWORDS

* ……………………
* ……………………
* ……………………

SYMBOLS

* ……………………
* ……………………
* ……………………

KINGS

The Kings of the court represent logic and understanding. They embody the element of Air and come to situations with clarity and knowledge. When Kings appear in a reading, we are being asked to embrace our ideas. They show us that our thoughts are not immature or fleeting, but well-founded and meaningful. We should not back down from using our ideas to build what we want and need.

KING OF PENTACLES

The King of Pentacles has used his knowledge to create a bounty, and is happy to share his abundance. Combining Air and Earth, he is dependable and generous, able to see who is in need, and secure in the knowledge that there will always be more. He is strong-willed and hardworking, but is smart enough to not let stubbornness get in the way of his success. When we pull the King of Pentacles, we should know our ideas will lead to success.

KEYWORDS	SYMBOLS
*	*
*	*
*	*

KING OF CUPS

The King of Cups, much like the Queen of Swords, embodies a healthy mind-heart connection that allows for deep understanding and compassion. Combining Air and Water, he brings intellect and logic into the emotional sphere. He is a diplomat, whose mastery of self-expression and benevolence makes him incredibly patient and supportive. When we see the King of Cups arise in a reading, we must bring out the patient, understanding parts of ourselves and come to situations from a place of kindness.

KEYWORDS	SYMBOLS
*	*
*	*
*	*

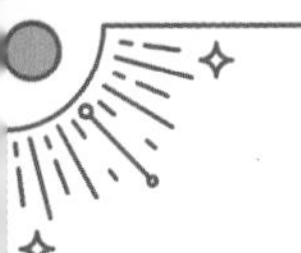

KING OF SWORDS

The King of Swords epitomizes the logic and intellect of all things Air. He can appear dispassionate or detached because he is so intently focused in the realm of thought. His advice comes from a place of deep wisdom, and his lack of caring is not generally malicious, but comes out of having such a sharp focus on the mind. When we see the King of Swords in a reading, we should embrace the rules and take our next steps using an abundance of logic and thought, secure in our ideas and our knowledge.

KEYWORDS	SYMBOLS
*	*
*	*
*	*

KING OF WANDS

The King of Wands combines passion and intelligence in a way that makes him incredibly charming while still authoritative. He is capable of creating any world that he can imagine with his intense drive. He brings Air to Fire, allowing his passion to move his ideas into reality. When the King of Wands is revealed during a reading, we should embrace our assets to accomplish our goals. He encourages us to use our creative spark and our ideas to be our most successful selves.

KEYWORDS	SYMBOLS
*	*
*	*
*	*

NAME GAME

Think of a person—it can be someone in your personal life, a historical figure, a celebrity, or a character from a book, movie, or television show—that you associate with the traits of each court card. Do not be overly concerned with age or gender: focus on the characteristics that connect you to each card.

Page of Pentacles ....

....

....

Page of Cups ....

....

....

Page of Swords ....

....

....

Page of Wands ....

....

....

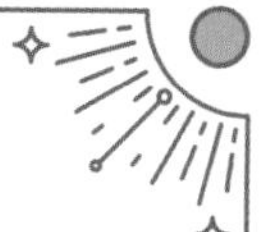

Knight of Pentacles

Knight of Cups

Knight of Swords

Knight of Wands

Queen of Pentacles

Queen of Cups

Queen of Swords

Queen of Wands

King of Pentacles

King of Cups

King of Swords

King of Wands

ACE TO 10

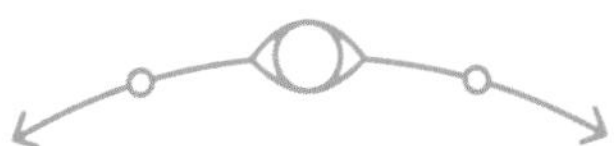

As we move from the court cards to the numeric cards, we see the evolution of each element cycle through the numbers one to ten. When we combine the element of the suit with the meaning of each number, we can understand where we are in specific aspects of our journeys. Understanding the characteristics of the numbers and how they relate to each suit will allow for clear meanings to come through in every reading. Just as the elements react to each other differently, certain numbers sit better in some suits than they do in others. Understanding the placements will show you why some cards are associated with positivity, while others are more difficult to contend with.

ACES

Aces bring us new opportunities, offering all the power of each element in its purest form. These cards are full of potential, pushing us forward toward fresh starts and exciting prospects. Their force can feel immature at times, with so much power and very little direction, but if we can wield their power and use it to our advantage, there is no limit to what can be accomplished.

ACE OF PENTACLES

The Ace of Pentacles represents new beginnings in the material world. With this card we are open to new possibilities in our health or finances. We may find ourselves at the start of a new path in life, and we should be encouraged to explore this path, as it can lead us toward prosperity.

KEYWORDS	SYMBOLS
* ________	* ________
* ________	* ________
* ________	* ________

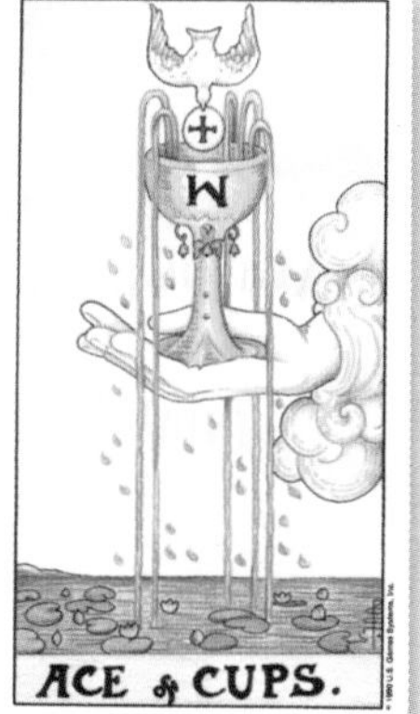

ACE OF CUPS

The Ace of Cups shows the new energy of an ace in your emotional life. This card can show us something new that we are meant to celebrate. It may be a relationship with another person, or a renewal of self-love that will allow you to approach the world with a revitalized openheartedness.

KEYWORDS	SYMBOLS
*	*
*	*
*	*

ACE OF SWORDS

The Ace of Swords gives us new ideas. When we pull this ace, we can expect breakthroughs that will give us clarity and insight, encouraging us to start projects with focus and determination. We can use the sword to cut through anything that may have been blocking us in the past.

KEYWORDS	SYMBOLS
*	*
*	*
*	*

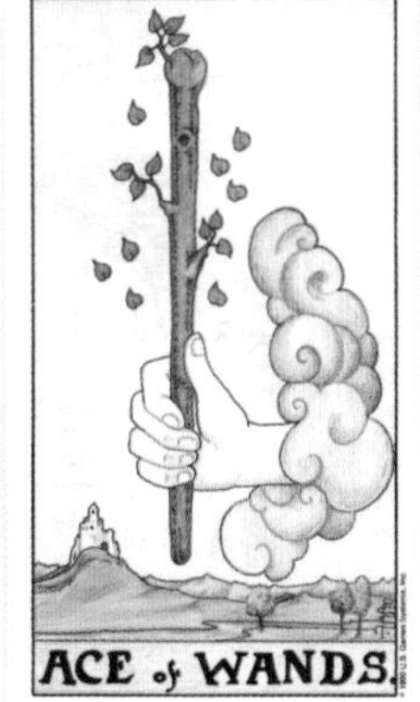

ACE OF WANDS

The Ace of Wands is pure energy. It is the spark of ambition, capable of driving your growth in whatever aspect of your life needs a push. When this ace comes up, we can think of it like a match, lighting a fire within us to start projects that excite us and tap into our full potential.

KEYWORDS	SYMBOLS
*	*
*	*
*	*

TWOS

Twos offer harmony. Like balanced scales, or a yin and yang, these cards show us the potential of each element when it is in equilibrium. They show us how even contrasting parts of life can work together in a solid partnership. This duality can sometimes indicate the need to make a decision, but the stability of the number gives us confidence in our choices.

TWO OF PENTACLES

The Two of Pentacles shows us how to bring stability and harmony to our day-to-day lives. This card reminds us to be flexible and allow ourselves to adapt to the things in our physical world that may be pulling us out of sync. This is the card of work-life balance and multitasking. The Two of Pentacles tells us that our material success will come from finding that balance.

KEYWORDS	SYMBOLS
* ______	* ______
* ______	* ______
* ______	* ______

TWO OF CUPS

The Two of Cups brings peace and harmony into our emotions, showing us what an ideal, mutually beneficial relationship can be. Each person in the relationship offers something the other lacks, and they grow together in a way that improves them both. This card represents two people who are in sync in every way. While not always a romantic relationship, this is always a healthy and satisfying one that runs deep.

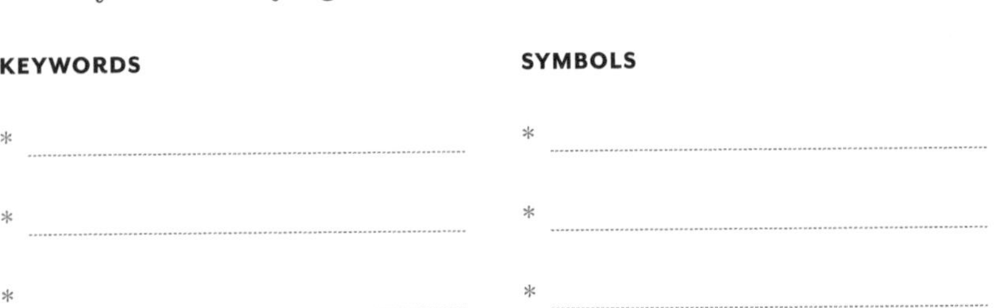

KEYWORDS	SYMBOLS
* ______	* ______
* ______	* ______
* ______	* ______

TWO OF SWORDS

The balance in the Two of Swords has landed us in a stalemate of sorts. Here, the energy of Air has given us choices, and we know we must make a decision about something that we may not have clarity on. The Two of Swords encourages us to cut through whatever is preventing us from seeing clearly so that we can move forward in the direction that will serve us best.

KEYWORDS

* ____________________
* ____________________
* ____________________
* ____________________
* ____________________

SYMBOLS

* ____________________
* ____________________
* ____________________
* ____________________
* ____________________

TWO OF WANDS

The Two of Wands shows us how to grow the initial spark of the ace and find ways to explore the world around us. This card confirms for us that decisions made with passion and excitement can lead us on a path of adventure that will show us how to bring new prospects to life.

KEYWORDS

* ____________________
* ____________________
* ____________________
* ____________________
* ____________________

SYMBOLS

* ____________________
* ____________________
* ____________________
* ____________________
* ____________________

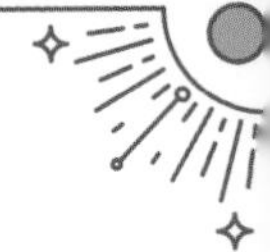

GIVE ME A HAND

The aces have more in common between the suits than any other cards in the deck. In the Rider-Waite deck, each ace is pictured as a hand coming out of the clouds, holding the symbol of its respective suit.

How do you relate this hand to the idea of new beginnings? Do you see this hand as an outside force offering you the symbol, or do you see it as your hand reaching out and grabbing it?

If you are not using a Rider-Waite deck, is there another symbol displayed across the cards? What does it mean to you?

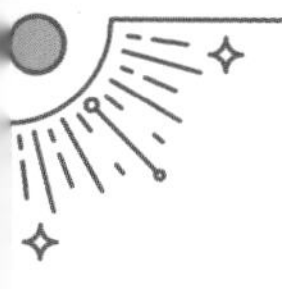
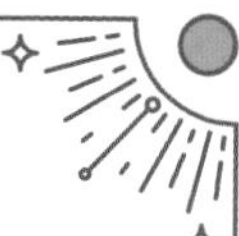

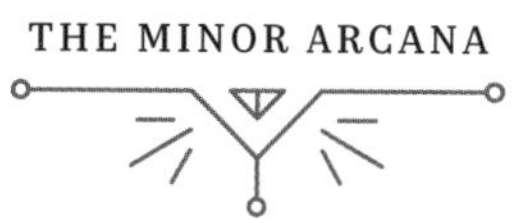

MAJOR/MINOR CONNECTION

In numerology, we add the digits of a number together to get to the meaning of the base number. The cards that represent the number two in the Major Arcana are the High Priestess (II), Justice (XI), and Judgement (XX). Draw lines between the Major and Minor Arcana twos you see strong connections between. Use the space to note what their connection means to you.

THREES

Threes give us insight into our development and can show us our creative potential. While aces start off the energy, and twos offer balance, threes allow for growth, as the energy of the element becomes more stable. We combine the previous numbers to form a group that allows us to manifest the things we need.

THREE OF PENTACLES

The Three of Pentacles brings us success in the material world, allowing the grounding force of the number to plant us solidly in places where we can thrive. When we see this card, we know that we are in a position to collaborate and use our skills to create anything we can imagine.

KEYWORDS	SYMBOLS
*	*
*	*
*	*
*	*

THREE OF CUPS

The Three of Cups is a card of joy and friendship. With this card, we are expanding emotionally, sharing our delight, and sharing in others' happiness. When the Three of Cups comes up in a reading, we have something to celebrate and should embrace the good in our lives.

KEYWORDS	SYMBOLS
*	*
*	*
*	*
*	*

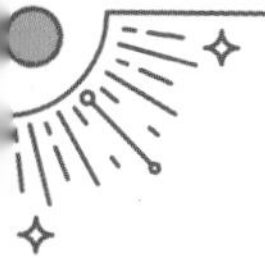

THREE OF SWORDS

The Three of Swords is a difficult card that can show us betrayal and sorrow. The stalemate that we found in the Two of Swords has shifted as we moved to three, and the growth we experience in this suit is a trying one. While this card can feel painful, it is not entirely hopeless. This card reminds us to keep moving forward to settle what is out of sorts.

KEYWORDS

*
*
*
*
*

SYMBOLS

*
*
*
*
*

THREE OF WANDS

The Three of Wands is surveying the possibilities of the future, prepared for whichever way the journey leads. This card shows us the fire in our belly and gives us the push we need in life. The growth of this card is a growth in our power. We may not know what the next step is, but once we make a decision and take that step, we can move with confidence.

KEYWORDS

SYMBOLS

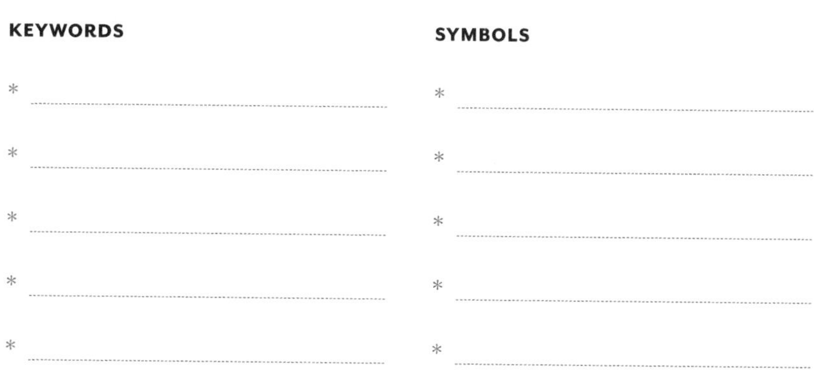

FOURS

With the fours, we arrive at the stable place that we have been working toward. This energy has us settled and secure in each element. If we set our intentions, we can use the structure that fours offer to manifest whatever our hearts desire.

FOUR OF PENTACLES

The Four of Pentacles brings stability to our material lives. We are being rewarded with abundance for the work that we have done. When this card comes up, we can expect to find stability financially, in our careers, or with our health. This is not yet a bounty we are willing to share, but it is one that sets us up for success.

KEYWORDS	SYMBOLS
*	*
*	*
*	*
*	*

FOUR OF CUPS

The Four of Cups offers us a chance to examine where we are emotionally. The waters are calm and so we can look inward to figure out what it is we need. We are being offered a cup, showing us that we can bring those emotional needs into our world if we just reach out.

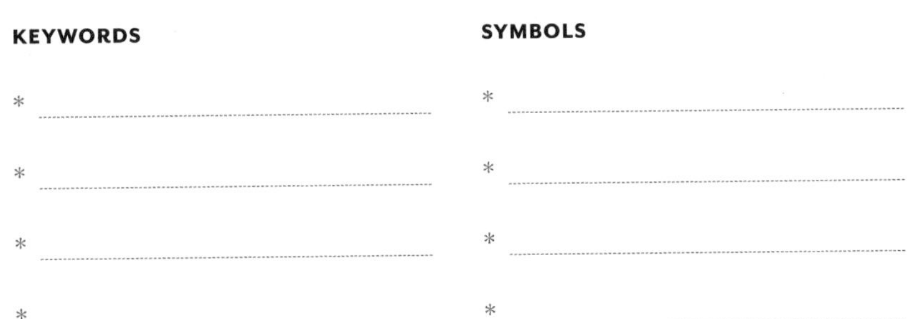

KEYWORDS	SYMBOLS
*	*
*	*
*	*
*	*

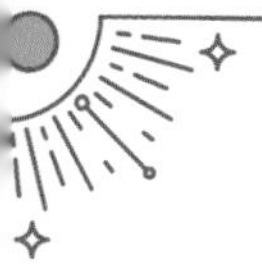

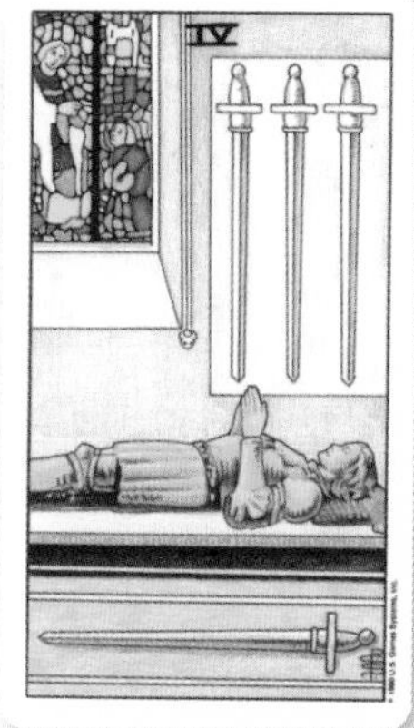

FOUR OF SWORDS

The Four of Swords gives us the chance to rest, take a deep breath, and meditate on what we need. This period of recuperation allows us to get out of our heads and let go of any thoughts that might be clouding our judgement or standing in our way. We should embrace this rest and allow ourselves this time so we can make room for new and clearer thoughts and ideas.

KEYWORDS

*
*
*
*
*

SYMBOLS

*
*
*
*
*

FOUR OF WANDS

The Four of Wands gives great energy to our stability, offering a beautiful picture of life. The image shows the four wands standing as supports or pillars that would support a structure: the power of this card gives us a foundation to build exactly what we want in life.

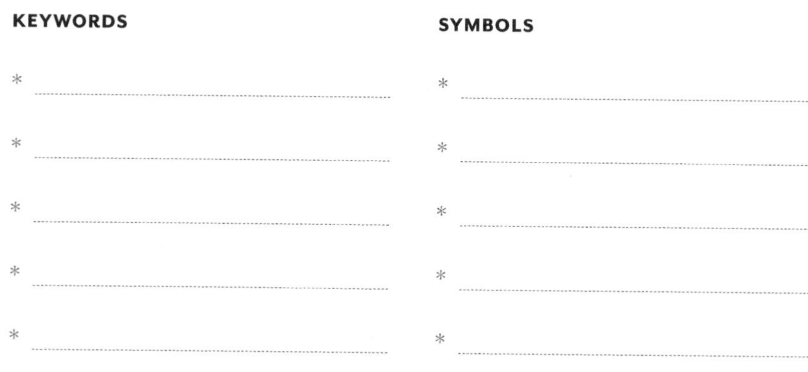

KEYWORDS

*
*
*
*
*

SYMBOLS

*
*
*
*
*

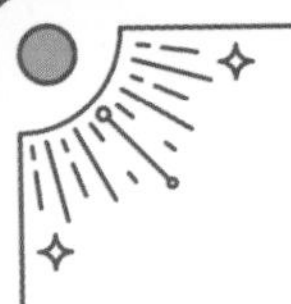

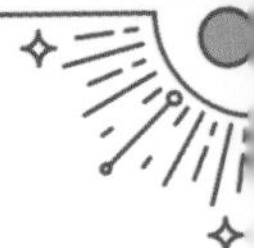

THREE'S COMPANY

The transition from ace to two to three is the first time we can see how different numbers in the same suit can work together. When we see progressions in spreads, we can look at how the numbers interact with each other to reinforce the meaning of the cards. What progression do you see in each suit as you move from ace to two to three? How is the story growing from card to card?

PENTACLES

CUPS

SWORDS

WANDS

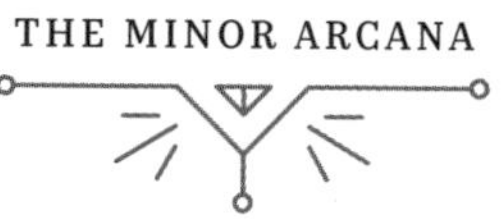

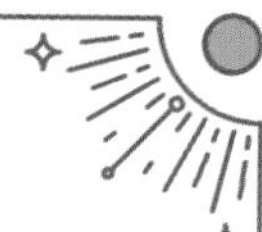

FAMOUS FOURSOMES

The number four comes up a lot in tarot reading and in life. In tarot, we have four suits, four elements, and four court cards. Come up with examples of foursomes in the world around you and sort them based on the card you relate to each.

FOURSOME:

FOURSOME:

FOURSOME:

FOURSOME:

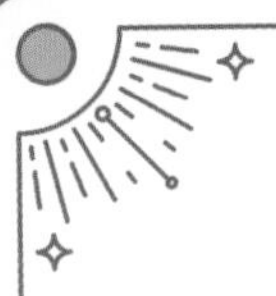

FIVES

Fives are difficult cards across all suits. They show us where we are facing challenges in our lives, exposing places of volatility, struggle, and disagreement. They encourage us to change, letting us know the areas where we need to shift our thinking or behavior to avoid getting stuck.

FIVE OF PENTACLES

The Five of Pentacles shows us hardship. We are isolated and in need of help, but we lack the resources we need to thrive. When this card appears, we must look at our physical world and identify where the hardships are coming from. Once we recognize these difficulties, we can start to make changes.

KEYWORDS

* ....
* ....
* ....
* ....

SYMBOLS

* ....
* ....
* ....
* ....

FIVE OF CUPS

The Five of Cups has a deep sadness that is immediately evident. This card shows struggle with our emotions, through regret, depression, or loss. If we are suppressing these emotions, we must face them. The figure on the card can only see the spilled cups; we must turn to see that which we still have, seeking change so that we can be fulfilled again.

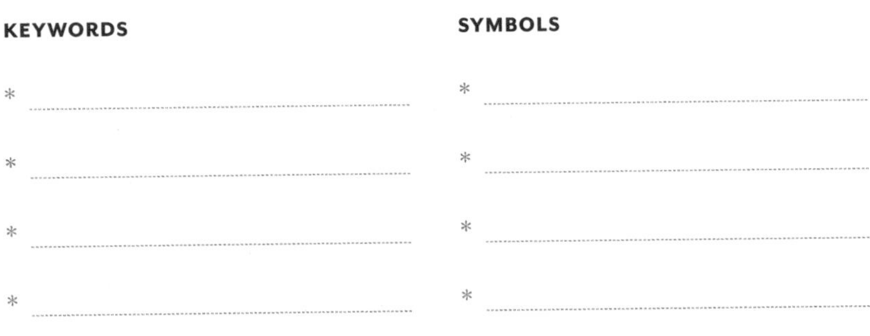

KEYWORDS

* ....
* ....
* ....
* ....

SYMBOLS

* ....
* ....
* ....
* ....

FIVE OF SWORDS

The Five of Swords is a card of conflict, showing betrayal and deceit. One side has emerged victorious over another, but the win is not a joyous one, and the defeat devastating. We may have been too quick to cut, and must evaluate how we can pick up the pieces after so much has been fractured.

KEYWORDS	SYMBOLS
*	*
*	*
*	*
*	*
*	*

FIVE OF WANDS

The Five of Wands brings misunderstandings. This card is another fighting card, but we are in the midst of the battle. The energy that the wands carry is being used in a clash. Our power is being wasted on this fight, and we must learn how to lower our weapons before we will be able to use this energy to move forward.

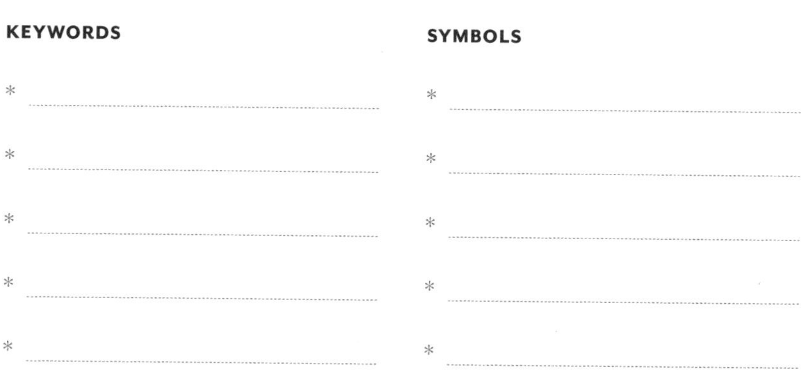

KEYWORDS	SYMBOLS
*	*
*	*
*	*
*	*
*	*

SIXES

With the sixes, we have a chance to recover from the difficulties we had with the fives. Here we are able to communicate freely. Our interactions are in harmony with others and with our true inner selves. As we start the second half of our cycle, we are starting from a place where we have learned to cooperate with the people around us in mutually beneficial ways.

SIX OF PENTACLES

The Six of Pentacles is a generous card. We have more than we need, and we see the value in helping others by sharing our abundance. This card encourages us to give back to our communities and the people around us.

KEYWORDS	SYMBOLS
*	*
*	*
*	*
*	*

SIX OF CUPS

The Six of Cups offers us simplicity and nostalgia for simpler times. We are reminded to look back to the times in our lives where our cups and hearts were full and tap into that fullness. We can share this fullness of love with those around us and bring forward the joy we've experienced in the past.

KEYWORDS	SYMBOLS
*	*
*	*
*	*
*	*

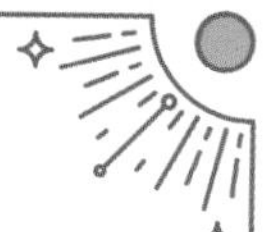

SIX OF SWORDS

The Six of Swords represents forward movement, away from difficult times. We are ready to move on from the troublesome parts of the past, with complete awareness of the situation we are removing ourselves from. We are beginning our transformation into the next part of our journey, prepared for whatever the road may bring.

KEYWORDS

*
*
*
*
*

SYMBOLS

*
*
*
*
*

SIX OF WANDS

The Six of Wands is a card of confidence, displaying a victory. We have figured out how to wield our power in a way that has led to a great success. This card shows us that we are on the correct path. Our accomplishments are recognized by those around us. We are embracing our ability to thrive through our own leadership.

KEYWORDS

SYMBOLS

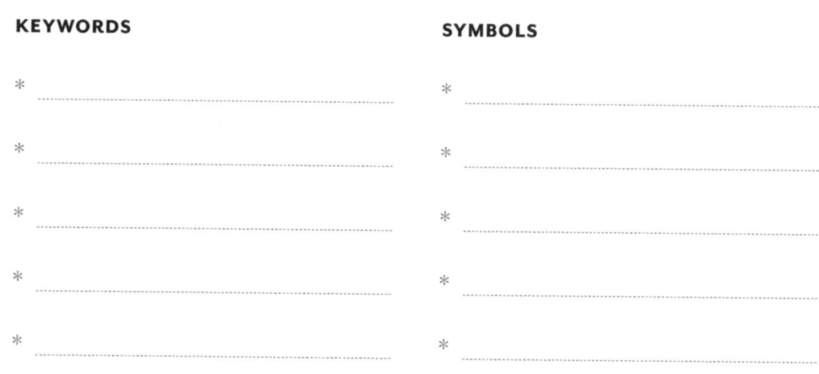

EMBRACING CHANGES

When we face the struggles that come with the fives, we must be prepared to make changes in our lives so that we may continue on our journeys. We have to release the difficulties and make room for better things to come to us.

In the areas governed by each suit below, write about how you could make changes that would result in a positive next step.

PENTACLES

CUPS

SWORDS

WANDS

THE LOVERS AND THE DEVIL

The sixes of the Major Arcana are represented by the Lovers (VI) and the Devil (XV). Each Minor Arcana six takes on attributes of both of these cards. What attributes of the Lovers and the Devil do you see in each of the sixes?

	THE LOVERS.	 THE DEVIL .
 VI (Six of Pentacles)	* …… * …… * ……	* …… * …… * ……
 VI (Six of Cups)	* …… * …… * ……	* …… * …… * ……
 VI (Six of Swords)	* …… * …… * ……	* …… * …… * ……
 VI (Six of Wands)	* …… * …… * ……	* …… * …… * ……

SEVENS

Sevens give us a chance to reflect on where we are and what we've learned. At this point in our journey, across all parts of our lives, we've seen victories and defeats, successes and failures, happiness and sorrow. Now we can take a step back to evaluate and take stock of what knowledge we've gained.

SEVEN OF PENTACLES

The Seven of Pentacles examines our long-term efforts in the physical world. When we see this card, we are being asked to be patient with these things, secure in the knowledge that there will be a reward, even though we are exhausted from the work we've had to do. We may be overwhelmed or buried by the amount of effort we've put in, but we are getting to a point where our perseverance will pay off.

KEYWORDS

* ______________________________
* ______________________________
* ______________________________

SYMBOLS

* ______________________________
* ______________________________
* ______________________________

SEVEN OF CUPS

The Seven of Cups asks us to reflect on where we are emotionally. Each cup represents a different aspect of life, so we are being asked to take a step back and examine how we are reacting to different parts of our lives from an emotional standpoint. With so much to consider, this card can feel overwhelming. We are reminded that we can't stay in that indecisive place for long.

KEYWORDS

* ______________________________
* ______________________________
* ______________________________

SYMBOLS

* ______________________________
* ______________________________
* ______________________________

SEVEN OF SWORDS

The Seven of Swords is a card of strategy. Up to this point, Swords have had the most difficult journey; reflecting on this can bring out our manipulative side. We do not want to have to go through the struggles that we've faced before, and we are willing to scheme to do whatever must be done. When we see this card, we must acknowledge how we are capable of deceit, and own up to our actions.

KEYWORDS	SYMBOLS
*	*
*	*
*	*
*	*
*	*

SEVEN OF WANDS

The Seven of Wands displays perseverance. At this point in our progression, we are steadfast in our beliefs and willing to fight for those beliefs. When we see this card, we are asked to stand up for ourselves. We will earn the respect of others by refusing to back down and by standing firm in what we know to be true.

KEYWORDS	SYMBOLS
*	*
*	*
*	*
*	*
*	*

EIGHTS

Eights give us the beginning of the end of each elemental cycle. We are approaching the strongest version of each element, and the eights shine a light on how we can use this strength to make changes that will propel us forward. Eights can offer challenges, but they are challenges that will lead to achievements, if we can take action in the trials we face. We are given as much time as we need in the number eight, and can use its infinite loop as a way to focus our energy on what we must learn here.

EIGHT OF PENTACLES

The Eight of Pentacles shows us the connection between hard work and our ambition. We are given the chance to use our earthly powers to reach our full potential, but to get there we must put in the work. With this card we are being asked to take on a lot. We must look at every part of a project, from the most minute of details to the big picture; nothing can be ignored.

KEYWORDS	SYMBOLS
*	*
*	*
*	*

EIGHT OF CUPS

The Eight of Cups asks us to make a sacrifice in order to move forward. We must trust that through this sacrifice we will be able to find more fulfillment, and focus on what lies ahead rather than what we might be leaving behind. If we can embrace this change, the rewards will be immense, and we cannot let fear of that loss stop us from moving forward.

KEYWORDS	SYMBOLS
*	*
*	*
*	*

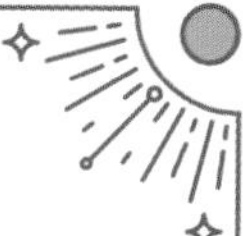

EIGHT OF SWORDS

The Eight of Swords shows us our vulnerability and our fears. Our thoughts are being clouded by these fears, and we feel trapped, unable to see a way forward. The action here must be releasing ourselves from our doubts so we don't remain stuck in this loop. We must open our eyes and use the power of the swords to cut through what's holding us in this place.

KEYWORDS

*
*
*
*
*

SYMBOLS

*
*
*
*
*

EIGHT OF WANDS

The Eight of Wands allows our energy to be in constant movement. Just as fire unconstrained can grow exponentially, our power has grown and we can use this card to channel even more energy toward whatever we are trying to manifest. With this card, we are being told that we can focus our attention on any goal and we will be able to achieve it.

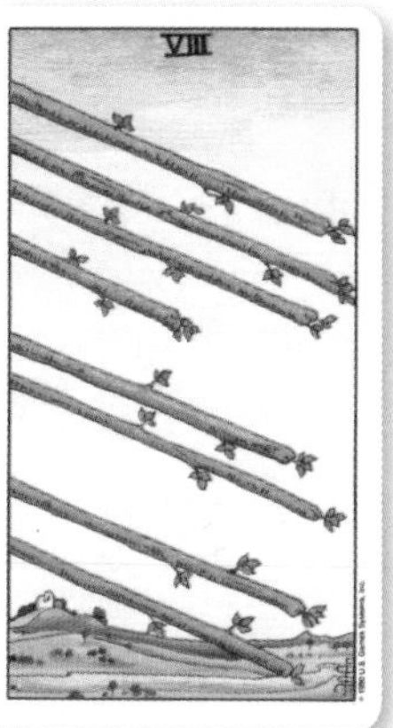

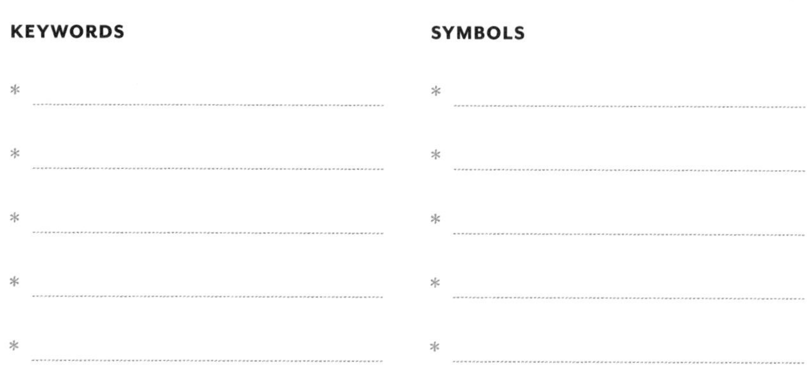

KEYWORDS

*
*
*
*
*

SYMBOLS

*
*
*
*
*

DRAW A SEVEN

Reflect on your understanding of the sevens. Pick one whose meaning you'd like to explore more and create your own version, using images and symbols that have particular resonance for you.

THE INFINITE 8

We can see from the symbol of 8 how easily energy and time can be devoted to this card. We must consciously make choices to move forward, otherwise the loop will continue interminably, as there is no start or end to the symbol. This can be beneficial when we need time to work on mastering a skill or channeling our inner strength, but difficult when we are stuck in situations where hard decisions have to be made.

Visualize the number 8 in each suit and mark up the number based on what you see. In which direction does the energy flow for you? Where do you see the entrance and exit points? With this exercise, when you find yourself stuck in an 8, you will be able to use this image to power your move forward.

PENTACLES

8

CUPS

8

SWORDS

8

WANDS

8

NINES

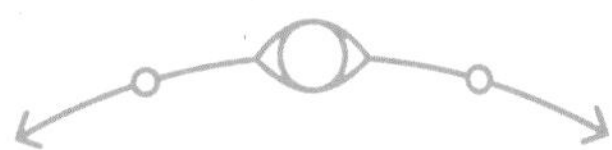

We have opened the eight and can see all of the power that each element has to offer. The nines are our last chance for action in this cycle. For some suits, this level of power can be welcome and fulfilling; for others, it can feel overwhelming to the point of despair. When we are given nines, we must embrace either side of the power and know that we are prepared for it. We've been through all the previous iterations of this energy and are capable of handling all that comes our way.

NINE OF PENTACLES

We've done the work and can allow our rewards to come to us in full force. Our crops are ready, and we've matured as much as our harvest has. The physical and earthly effort we put in up to this point is paying off, and we are open to receiving the abundance that we worked so hard for.

KEYWORDS	SYMBOLS
*	*
*	*
*	*

NINE OF CUPS

The Nine of Cups offers us emotional fulfillment and pleasure. We have found true happiness, and having been through previous turmoil it is all the sweeter. We are flooded with joy and light, and see that any sacrifices we made and heartaches we suffered have led us to this point of perfect alignment and serenity.

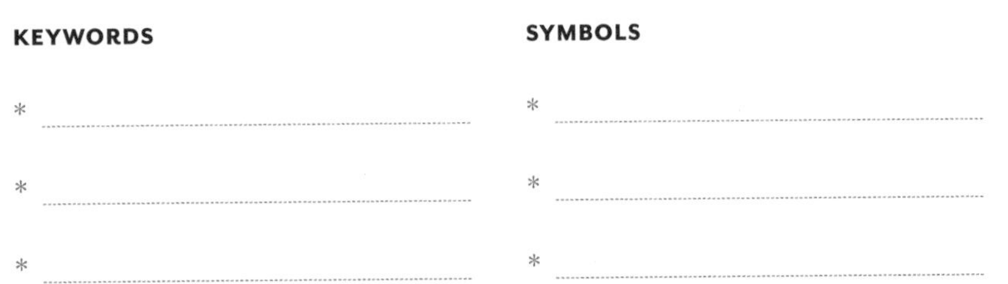

KEYWORDS	SYMBOLS
*	*
*	*
*	*

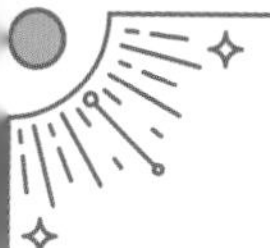

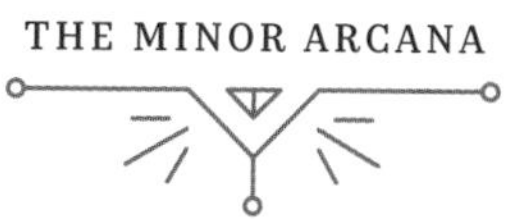

NINE OF SWORDS

The Nine of Swords displays all of the power of Swords, and their intensity can feel crushing. This is a card full of our anxieties. When this card is pulled, we need to look at the things that we are obsessing over that are causing despair. This fixation is fueling our nightmares, which can then escape into our daily life. There is no easy way out here: the only way to the other side is through.

KEYWORDS

*
*
*
*
*

SYMBOLS

*
*
*
*
*

NINE OF WANDS

The Nine of Wands is a card of determination. Here we can embrace fire's persistence in ways that allow us to move through any obstacle. The path may not be easy, and there may be destruction along the way, but when we pull this card, we know that we have the focus and drive to get through.

KEYWORDS

*
*
*
*
*

SYMBOLS

*
*
*
*
*

TENS

Tens are the final number of the Minor Arcana. With these cards, we close out the cycle of the suit and prepare to restart, taking with us all that we have learned in the previous progression. Numerologically, tens and aces are the same, so we must recognize that every end also serves as a new beginning.

TEN OF PENTACLES

The Ten of Pentacles offers us complete security and strength in all aspects of our material surroundings. With this card, we have an abundance that not only serves us, but allows us to provide support to those around us. This card is stable enough to connect us to ancestors and provide for our future selves and generations.

KEYWORDS	SYMBOLS
*	*
*	*
*	*
*	*

TEN OF CUPS

The Ten of Cups gives us emotionally what the Ten of Pentacles offered materially. Here we have an unshakeable emotional stability. Our relationships have reached a blissful maturity. Our heart is in alignment with the heart or hearts of others that can allow for a perfect harmony. We can be open-hearted in all matters, knowing that we are safe.

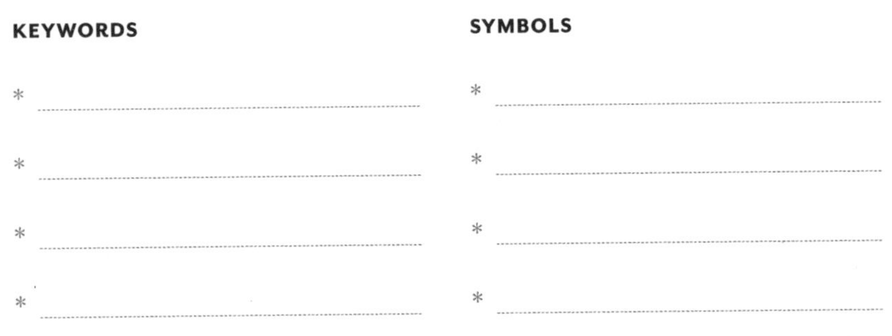

KEYWORDS	SYMBOLS
*	*
*	*
*	*
*	*

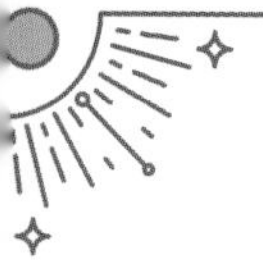
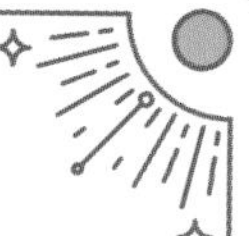

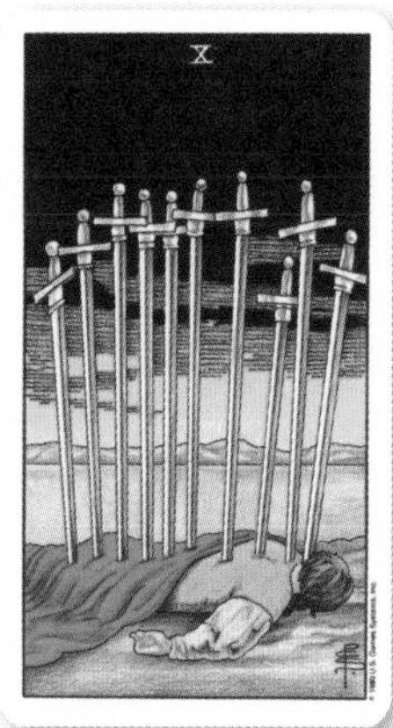

TEN OF SWORDS

The Ten of Swords represents a devastating loss or betrayal. When we receive this card, we are forced to process what has hurt us so that we can move back to the start. As painful as this loss may be, we can take comfort in the fact that the difficulty is over now. We must use the swords to cut the ties that have hurt us so that we may make room to begin anew.

KEYWORDS

*
*
*
*
*

SYMBOLS

*
*
*
*
*

TEN OF WANDS

The Ten of Wands lays all the burden of power on our shoulders. We've come this far wielding this energy and cannot shy away from the responsibilities that come with the actions we have taken. This card is a reminder of our duties to others and our call to remember what our obligations are as we transition to new beginnings.

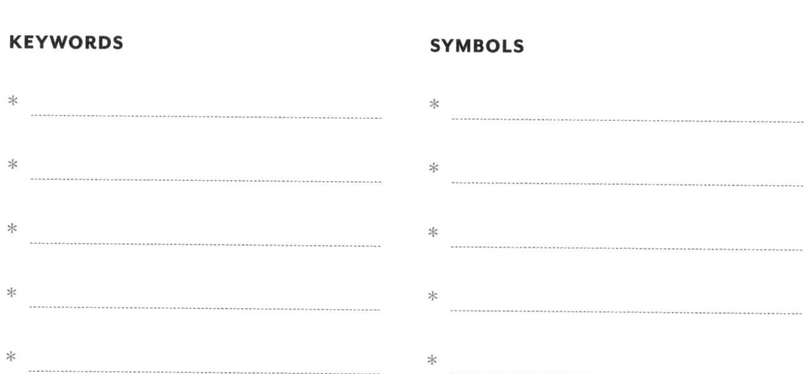

KEYWORDS

*
*
*
*
*

SYMBOLS

*
*
*
*
*

TAROT MATH

When we see multiple cards of the same suit in a reading, we are drawn to pay special attention to that suit. Sometimes, adding the numbers of the cards together can show us a new side of the card they add up to. Review the keywords linked to the smaller cards that add up to nine in each suit, and write some of the keywords from each that enhance your understanding of the nine.

PENTACLES

+

*
*
*

+

*
*
*

+

*
*
*

+

*
*
*

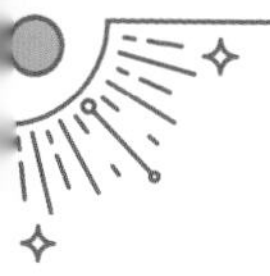

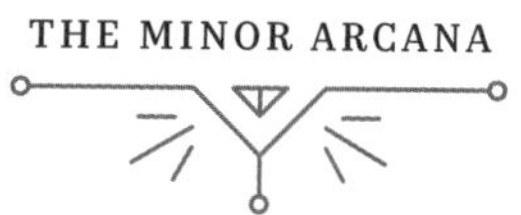

CUPS

+

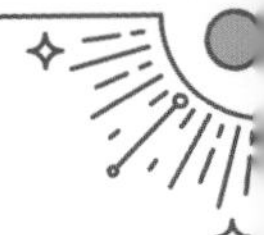

SWORDS

*

*

*

+

*

*

*

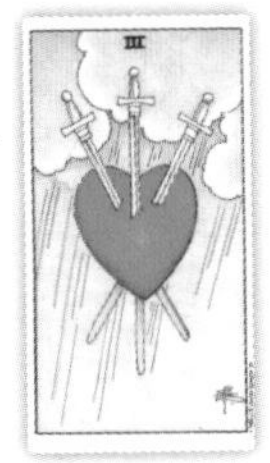

+

*

*

*

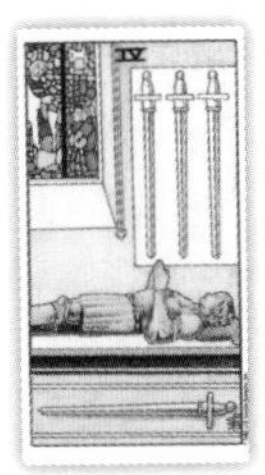

+

*

*

*

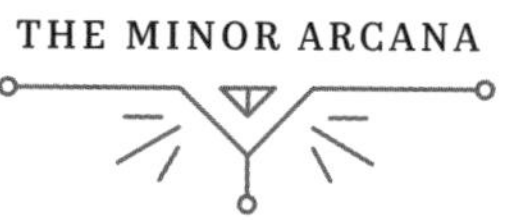
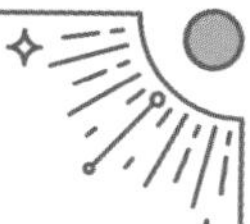

WANDS

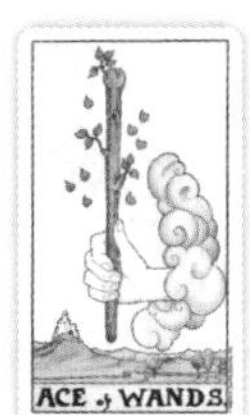

+

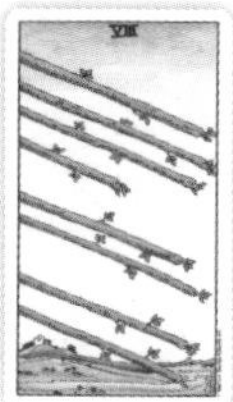

*
*
*

+

*
*
*

+

*
*
*

+

*
*
*

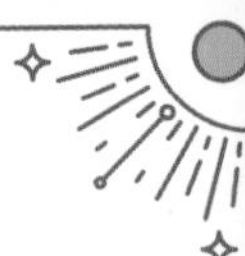

RESTARTING THE CYCLE

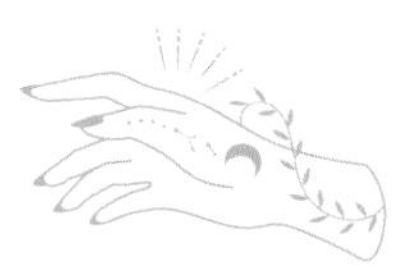

Once we reach a ten in any suit, we know that we are prepared to take what we've learned in that cycle and move on to a new journey, starting over at ace. Because of the cyclical nature of our lives, the ten is just as close to the ace as are any consecutive numbers. Using what you know about tens and aces, describe the transition from ten to ace in each suit.

PENTACLES

CUPS

SWORDS

WANDS

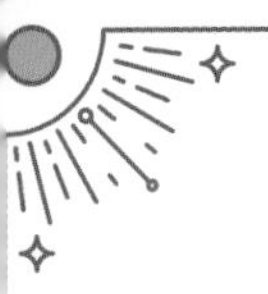
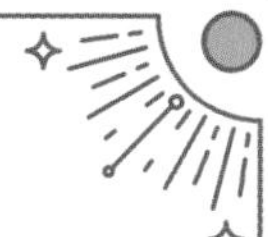

REVISITING THE SUITS

Now that you have an understanding of the journey of the cards through each suit, has your understanding of the suit changed? Do you have a clearer idea of the parts of your life that relate to each suit?

PENTACLES

CUPS

SWORDS

WANDS

tarot spreads

Tarot card spreads can range from simple to complex. Part of your understanding of the messages you'll receive from the cards will come from the questions that you ask, and how the cards present themselves to you. There is no one correct way to pull cards. Trusting your intuition is just as important in setting up a spread as it is in reading the cards themselves.

HOW TO READ SPREADS

Using spreads will allow you to find multifaceted answers to what you are looking to learn. Each reading will give you the chance to ask a major question and receive responses that narrow down those questions or point you to a specific part of the answer.

A deck can be a tool that allows you to see some of your innermost truths. The more comfortable you can get handling the cards, the easier it will be to see yourself reflected in the cards. Taking time while shuffling, learning the unique powers of a particular deck, understanding how to read various spreads, and seeing how different cards react with each other will allow you to get the most out of your cards.

The activities in this section will allow you to gain that comfort with the cards, ask illuminating questions, learn a few basic spreads, and learn how to create your own spreads.

SHUFFLING

Shuffle the deck while you think about the question(s) you will be asking. Take as much time as you need while shuffling to focus on the session and release any distractions. Do not let your shuffling abilities distract from connecting with the cards. Mixing the cards facedown on your reading space is just as effective as any advanced shuffling technique.

While mixing up the order of the cards matters, the real objective is imbuing the cards with your energy and intentions. Meditate on your connection to the deck, and instinct will tell you when to stop shuffling. Many people will cut the cards before they begin reading. If you are reading for someone other than yourself, you can let them do some shuffling and have them cut the deck so that their energy is drawn into the cards.

JUMPING CARDS

If you have been around tarot readers before, you may have heard the phrase "what falls to the floor comes to the door." Sometimes when you're shuffling, a card or two will "jump" out of the deck. For many, these cards are given special attention. You can address these cards individually, or incorporate them as the first pull of your spread.

Reading these cards separate from your spread can give insight into a question you might not even have known to ask. If it feels important enough, you can use that card as the basis for its own reading, continuing to shuffle while focused on that card, and asking for clarity on the message.

These cards may also be used to set the tone of the spread that you had already planned. You can place the card above where you plan to place the rest of the cards, and see if its interactions with the other cards gives more insight to your reading.

If the card feels like it should be the start of the spread that you had been planning, place it in the position of the spread that you're drawn to and continue dealing out the rest of the spread. The message in this card might end up having more meaning or weight than the others in the spread.

If you're skeptical about the meaning behind a jumping card, you can shuffle it back into the deck and continue as you were. It's worth noting what card it was—sometimes it will appear in the spread in another way; if not, you can see if it would have any effect on how you read, in case that changes your mind about them in the future.

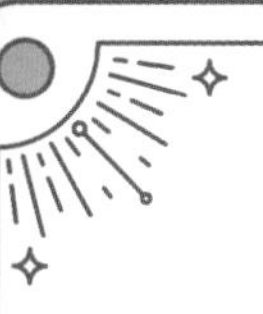
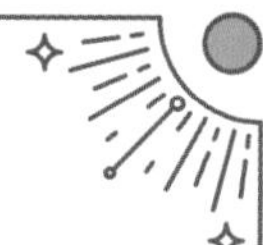

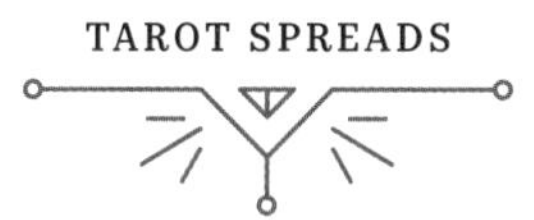

REVERSALS

A reversal is when you draw a card upside-down as you pull it from the deck. Deciding whether or not to read reversals is a personal decision that you can make as you work with your cards and learn how to interpret their messages. Trust your gut when it comes to making this decision, and remember that over time you can always change how you view this. If you have multiple decks, you may find that some are more suited to reading reversals than others. Some people completely ignore reversals, and always read the cards by their upright meanings, while others will see reversals as a way to get additional information from their cards.

Many decks have different meanings for each card based on whether it is pulled upright or reversed. Understanding the reversed meanings can be a great place to start interpreting more information from each pull. You can simply look up the reversed meaning of the card, plus your own interpretation if symbols appear to you differently in the reverse, as you would with the card upright.

Another option for reading reversed cards is understanding that their reversed meaning is showing you a path toward their upright meaning. This may be their way of showing you where your energy is blocked, and what steps you must take in that part of your life to take steps forward.

You may also choose to look at any display of a card as representative of all parts of that card. Each card may have both positive and negative aspects, and by acknowledging their duality, we can gain greater insight into all of the possibilities being shown to us. It can be our reminder that even the darkest days have a silver lining, and that there may be potential for problems in the best of times.

As you go through this chapter, see how often reversals come up for you and which of these methods makes the most sense to you intuitively.

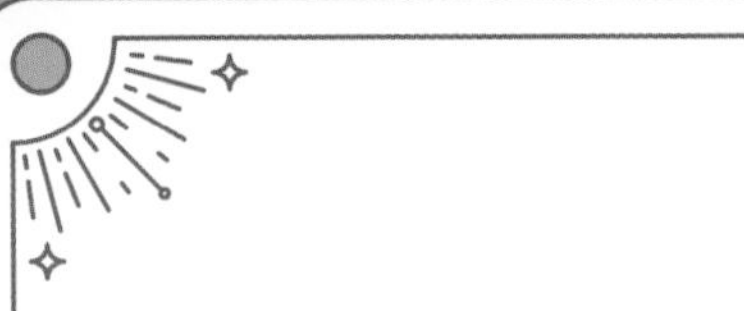

GETTING TO KNOW YOUR DECK

One of the first spreads that can be helpful for becoming familiar with a new deck is a deck interview. Rather than asking for questions about yourself, asking the deck for answers about itself can be enlightening as a way to introduce you to the cards, as well as give you a chance to practice a simple spread. A deck interview is also a great way to become familiar with reading cards and understanding how their meanings answer specific questions. There are many different deck interview spreads available. The following is a basic one that will give you a lot of information about using your deck.

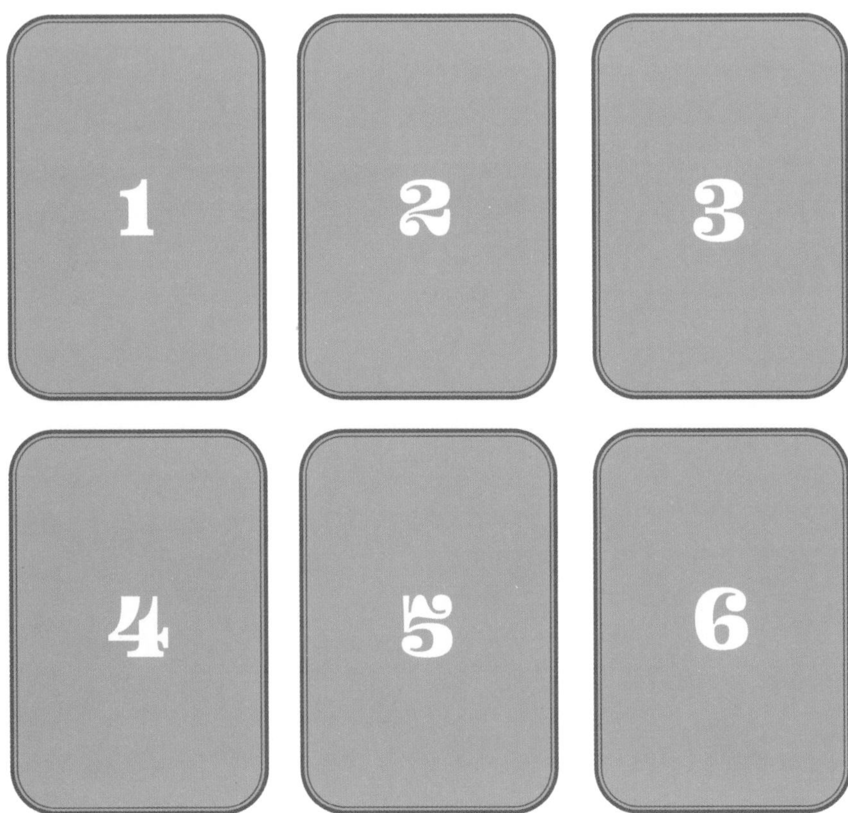

Shuffle your deck, keeping the interview questions in your mind as you do. When you feel ready, pull the cards. As you pull each card one by one, ask yourself the following questions in order, reflecting on the answers suggested by the cards.

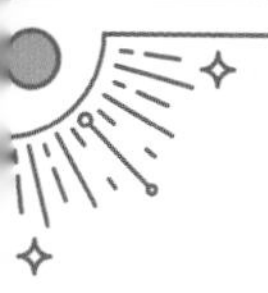

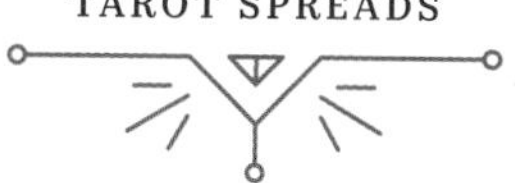

Name of Deck

1. What are your most important characteristics?

2. How can I best use your insights?

3. What are your strengths?

4. What are your weaknesses?

5. **What will you teach me about myself?**

6. **What will be the result of our work together?**

After you've asked these questions, it's important to take a look at how they work together. The meanings of cards can be maximized or minimized by their relationship to the cards around them. Take special care to note how the strengths and weaknesses of the deck play off of each other and what the transition from using the deck's insights to the result of the work might look like.

7. **What have I learned about my deck from this interview?**

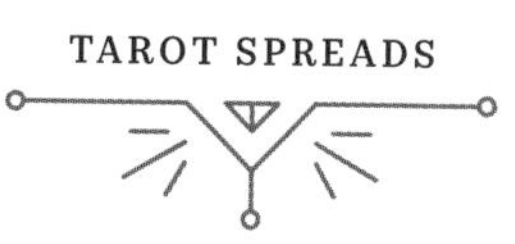

EXAMPLE DECK INTERVIEW

THE EMPEROR

This deck is authoritative and ambitious. It wants its advice to be recognized and respected. It will provide knowledge and guidance and can serve to lead me through difficulties.

STRENGTH

This deck will be best used if I can access my inner strength and use that to guide my readings and actions. It is encouraging me to trust my power and insights.

NINE OF CUPS

This deck's strengths are in finding my physical and emotional well-being. It wants me to be successful and will help me find contentment and happiness.

SEVEN OF CUPS

This deck's weaknesses fall within the realm of what-ifs. This deck will not help me make decisions if I am not ready to go forward with a plan. This deck wants me to put the work in; it will not advise me if I'm not ready to do the work.

TEN OF PENTACLES

This deck is in the position to teach me how to find professional success and stability and make sure that my work will be rewarded.

THE TOWER

Working with this deck can lead to major life changes. It will take me out of my comfort zone and into something completely new.

CONCLUSION

This deck is a powerful one, which will be especially helpful in matters of career and material success. This deck wants me to feel empowered by my inner self and be prepared to follow through on choices and take action. It can help me through major and powerful life changes. I should consult this deck while moving forward in those matters, but will not try to have it make decisions for me.

FORMULATING QUESTIONS

There are two parts to the questions you'll ask when you start reading your deck.

The first part is formulating the overall question. The most insightful readings happen when the questions are specific, positively framed, action based, and present-focused. Asking for specific actions will give you a way to move forward, rather than sitting in the space you currently occupy. Phrasing the question in a positive light will prevent the negativity you're holding onto about a situation from entering the reading and holding you back from the best possible outcome.

Using the following question starters as a guide, write some questions that you'd like to see answered by your tarot cards. Come up with some questions in each area of your life on the following pages.

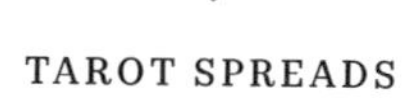
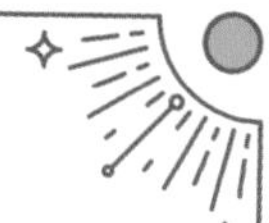

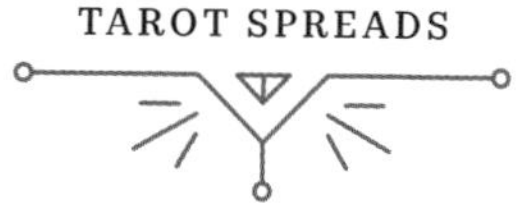

EMOTIONAL

Emotional questions should focus on relationships—family, friendships, romantic, or your relationship to yourself can all fall under this category.

* ....
* ....
* ....
* ....
* ....
* ....
* ....
* ....
* ....

PHYSICAL

Physical questions should focus on matters of the material world. These can be health-related, money-related, or questions about your relationship to the earth. This is a broad category, so give yourself room to stretch these questions to all corners of your life.

* ....
* ....
* ....
* ....
* ....
* ....
* ....
* ....
* ....

PASSION

Passion questions can help you tap into your creativity. Focus on the endeavors in your life you are passionate about. Form your questions around the fires that drive your vision.

* ______________________________
* ______________________________
* ______________________________
* ______________________________
* ______________________________
* ______________________________
* ______________________________
* ______________________________
* ______________________________

INTELLECTUAL

Intellectual questions can open your mind to deeper understanding. Use this space for questions relating to thoughts and understanding, and how those extend to your actions.

* ______________________________
* ______________________________
* ______________________________
* ______________________________
* ______________________________
* ______________________________
* ______________________________
* ______________________________
* ______________________________

The second part of formulating your question is picking the pieces of the answer that you are looking for. The most useful and accurate readings happen when you know exactly what the card you're pulling is telling you. Asking for each specific card or grouping of cards to correspond to one part of an answer, rather than doing an open-ended read of the cards, will give you a more specific path for moving forward.

SELF	**OBSTACLES**	**OUTSIDE FORCES**
PAST	**SOLUTIONS**	**STRENGTHS**
PRESENT	**OPTIONS**	**WEAKNESSES**
FUTURE	**HOPES**	**PROBLEMS**
INNER TRUTH	**FEARS**	**ACTIONS**
HIDDEN POTENTIAL	**DECISIONS**	**POSSIBLE OUTCOME**
WANTS	**NEEDS**	**CHANGES**

YES OR NO QUESTIONS

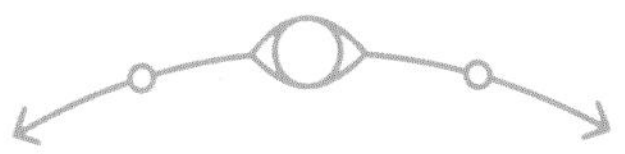

The simplest tarot reading you can learn is a single card pull, used to answer yes or no questions. These readings tend to give you more than just a simple yes or no. They can offer "yes, because . . ." or "no, because . . ." if you have an understanding of the cards.

While some cards may seem very obviously negative or positive, many cards are more ambiguous, and the subject matter of the question may affect how you'd read the answer. Even traditionally negative cards can be read as a "yes" if they relate directly to the question being asked. For example, while a card like Death may have negative connotations, if your question was about a major life change or an end to something, Death can be there to confirm what you're asking.

Meditate on a yes or no question. As before, the question will be best if it is specific, positive, and action-based. Write the question in the space provided and shuffle the deck as you think about it. Pull a single card. Write down the card and note if it's a yes or no. Go into further detail—why do you think this? What further messages are you receiving regarding the answer? Repeat this a few times to get a feel for how these readings work.

QUESTION ....

CARD ....

YES OR NO ....

WHY? ....

....

....

....

QUESTION

CARD

YES OR NO

WHY?

QUESTION

CARD

YES OR NO

WHY?

QUESTION

CARD

YES OR NO

WHY?

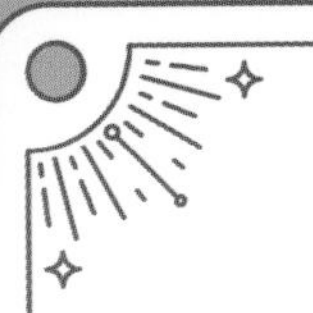

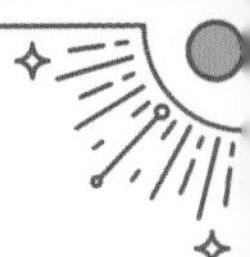

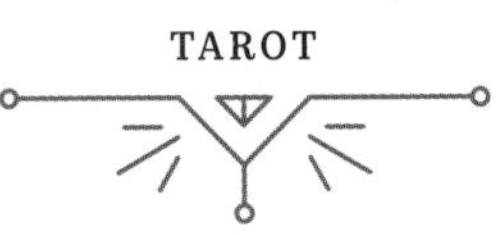

PULL A SINGLE CARD

Questions beyond yes or no can be answered by a single card as well. This is where those specific questions will allow you to get the most out of the card. Take your time with these pulls—there is a lot of information you can get from a single card. Beyond the standard meaning of the card, focus on the symbolism in the art, the meaning the number of the card might have for you, the element associated with the suit, and anything else that stands out to you on the card.

Write your question in the space provided. Shuffle your cards while you think about the question. When you feel ready, stop shuffling and pull a card. Write the card and your interpretation of how that card answers your question. Take into consideration the traditional meaning of the card, as well as any additional personal significance the card holds for you. Repeat this process with a few more questions.

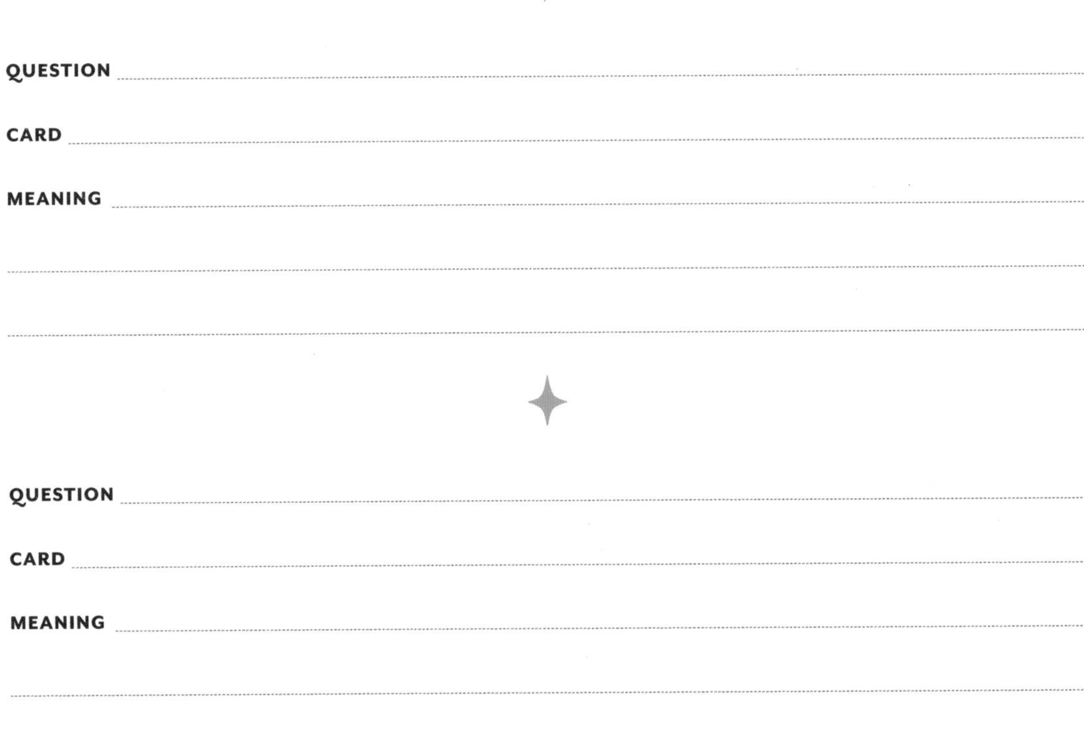

QUESTION ....

CARD ....

MEANING ....

....

....

QUESTION ....

CARD ....

MEANING ....

....

....

QUESTION

CARD

MEANING

QUESTION

CARD

MEANING

QUESTION

CARD

MEANING

QUESTION

CARD

MEANING

CARD-A-DAY JOURNAL

A single card can be pulled at the beginning of a day, week, or month and used as a predictor of what's to come. Remember that all cards have both negative and positive aspects to them, and pulling a "negative" card does not necessarily equate to having a bad day. Difficult cards can give us insight into what we might need to work on, or something that might come up that we will have to deal with. If you are working on a daily, weekly, or monthly practice, keeping a journal of which cards come up is a great way to expand your understanding both of tarot and of yourself. Repeated cards, numbers, or suits can give insight into what the focus of your energy should be over time.

Over the next week, at the start of your day, pick a single card. Meditate on it, and use the space provided to write down the card and what you think that will indicate for the day. At the end of the day, return to this book and write about an experience that related to that card. Was it what you expected based on your morning prediction? Or did something happen relating to an aspect of the card you didn't think about before? At the end of week, examine the journey of the cards over the course of the week. Were there any specific cards that repeated themselves? Suits that occurred with prominence?

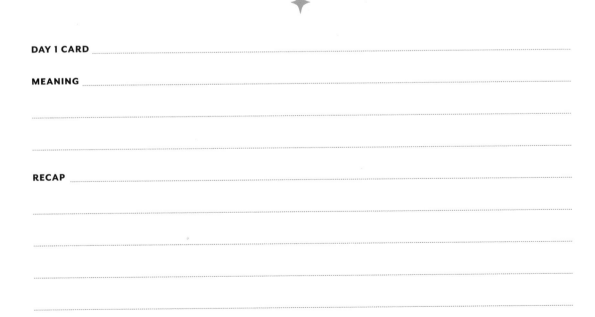

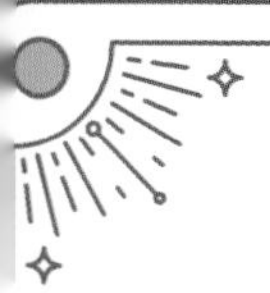

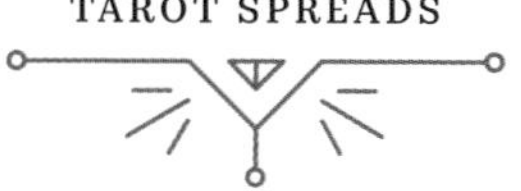

DAY 2 CARD

MEANING

RECAP

DAY 3 CARD

MEANING

RECAP

DAY 4 CARD

MEANING

RECAP

DAY 5 CARD

MEANING

RECAP

DAY 6 CARD

MEANING

RECAP

DAY 7 CARD

MEANING

RECAP

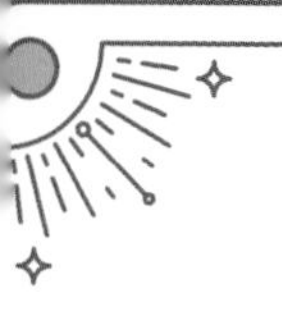

END OF THE WEEK REVIEW:

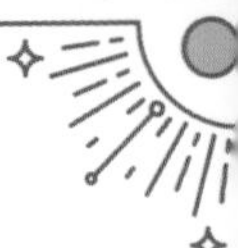

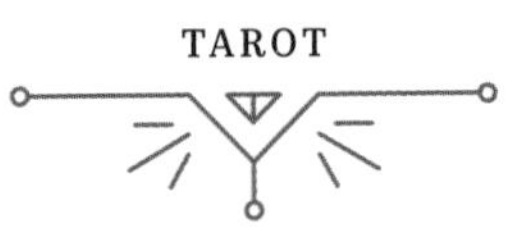

ONE TO THREE

The easiest way to move from a one-card pull to a three-card spread is to pull two additional cards to see what the single card is influenced by. Start with the same type of specific question that you would ask for a single-card pull. Once you've pulled the first card, ask for clarity on it. As you read the cards, take in their meaning individually, and then see how they interact with each other. Do they seem to be in agreement, or are they giving conflicting messages? Are any numbers or suits recurring?

If it feels more natural to you to swap the second and third card positions, the spread will be equally effective.

Shuffle the cards as you meditate on your question. Pull the cards and use the space provided to note the cards, their meanings pertaining to the question, and how the second and third cards relate to the first.

QUESTION ....

CARD 1 ....

MEANING ....

....

....

CARD 2

EFFECT ON CARD 1

CARD 3

EFFECT ON CARD 1

Write any additional notes here. Were there any similar suits? Numbers? Symbols? How do those affect how your question was answered?

PRACTICE A THREE-CARD SPREAD

Three-card spreads can be great for showing you different parts of an answer or giving you different options for solving a problem. The important thing to remember when you start pulling multiple-card spreads is to plan in advance, so as you pull each card, your intention for that card is something you've been concentrating on.

A lot of information can be gathered from a simple spread like the one above.

- Past—Present—Future
- Solution 1—Solution 2—How to Decide
- Desire—Obstacle—Action to Move Forward
- Problem—Solution—Unseen Difficulty
- Strengths—Weaknesses—Hidden Potential

Pick one of these three-card spreads and write in the card outlines on the next page which card will represent which parts of the answer. Write your question, shuffle your cards while thinking about the question, then write which card was pulled in each position and your interpretation of them.

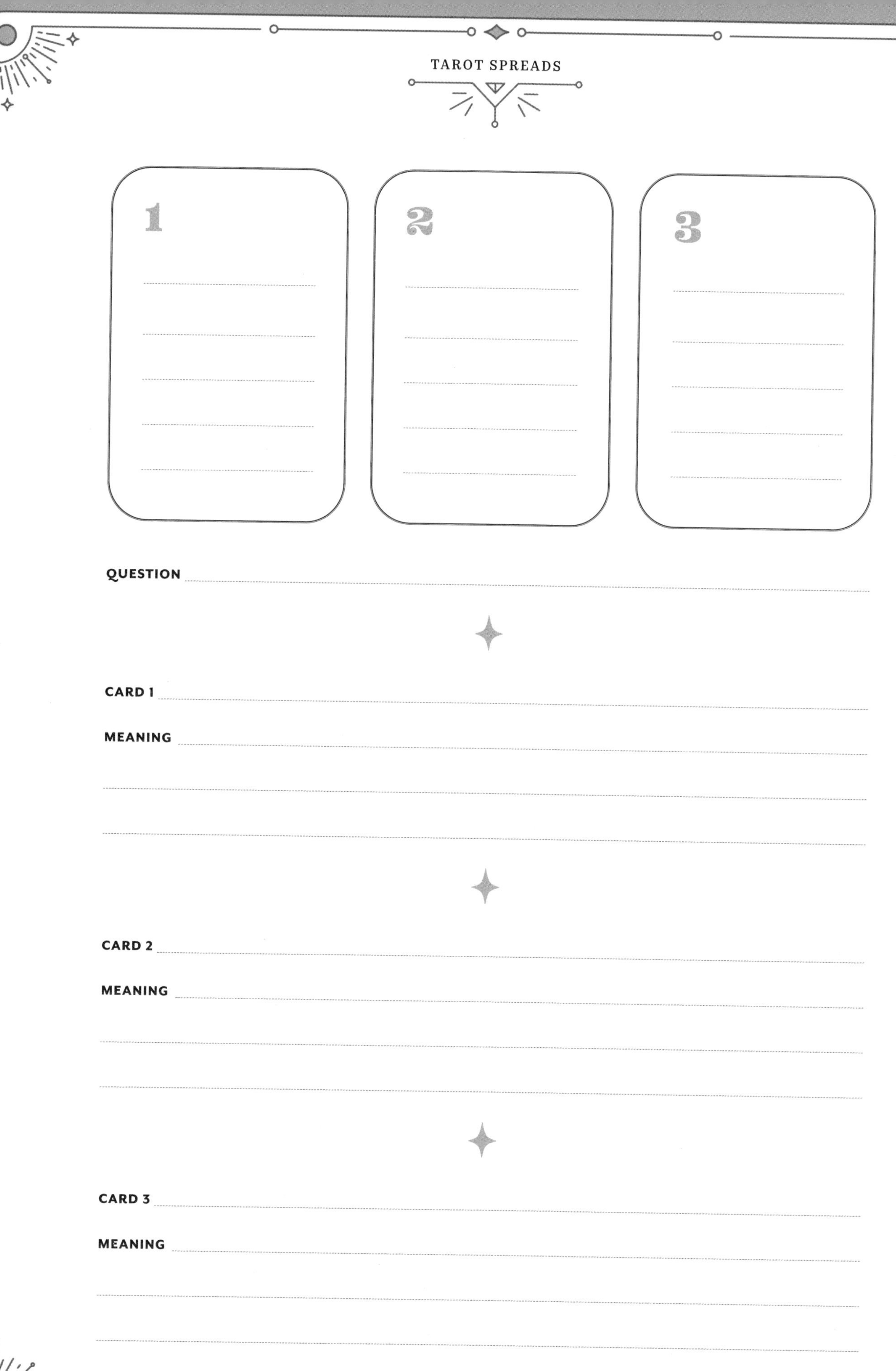

QUESTION

CARD 1

MEANING

CARD 2

MEANING

CARD 3

MEANING

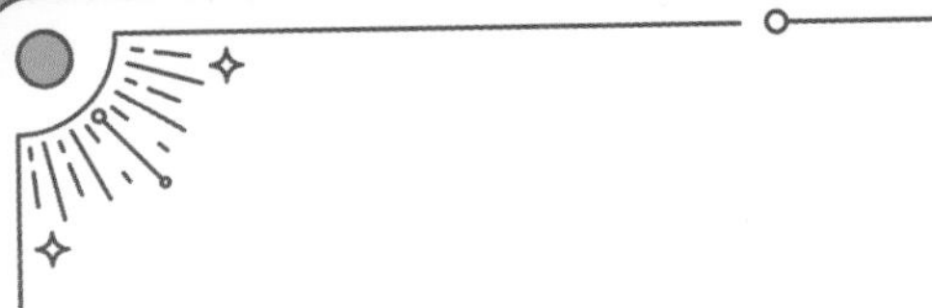

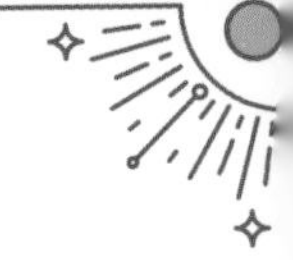

CREATE YOUR OWN THREE-CARD SPREAD

Once you've practiced a few three-card spreads, think about specific answers you would like to see to a question that you have. Indicate below which order you will pull the cards in, and which part of the answer will go with each card. Then read your cards using your new spread.

#	#	# ....
....	....	....
....	....	....
....	....	....
....	....	....
....	....	....

QUESTION ....

CARD 1 ....

MEANING ....

....

....

....

....

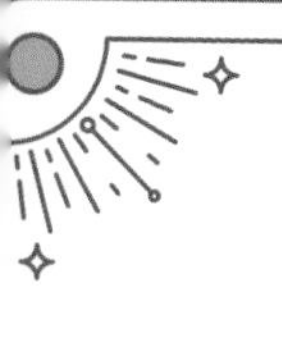

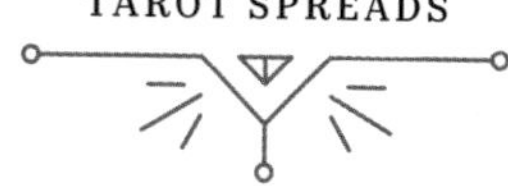

CARD 2 ....

MEANING ....

CARD 3 ....

MEANING ....

FACEUP OR FACEDOWN

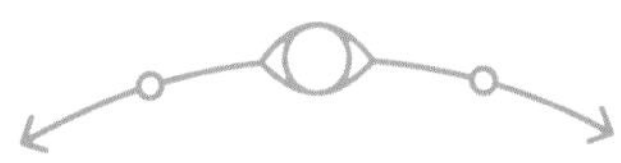

Once you start reading multiple-card spreads, you can decide to set up the spreads with cards facedown, reading them one at a time, or you can choose to place them faceup, to get a full view of the reading before looking at each one individually. Both processes have value, and it's worth trying each to see what feels more natural. You may find your preference changes based on the spread, deck, or any other variables of a specific reading. Here, you'll experiment with both methods to explore how they work for you, using a simple three-card spread of your choice.

First, lay out a spread with the cards facedown. Turn each one over based on the order called for by the specific spread you're using. This method can work well for really learning the meaning of each card individually, and understanding the message of the reading one piece at a time. Once you've taken in the cards individually, you can see how they interact with each other and if any additional messages are clear from the overall connections of the cards.

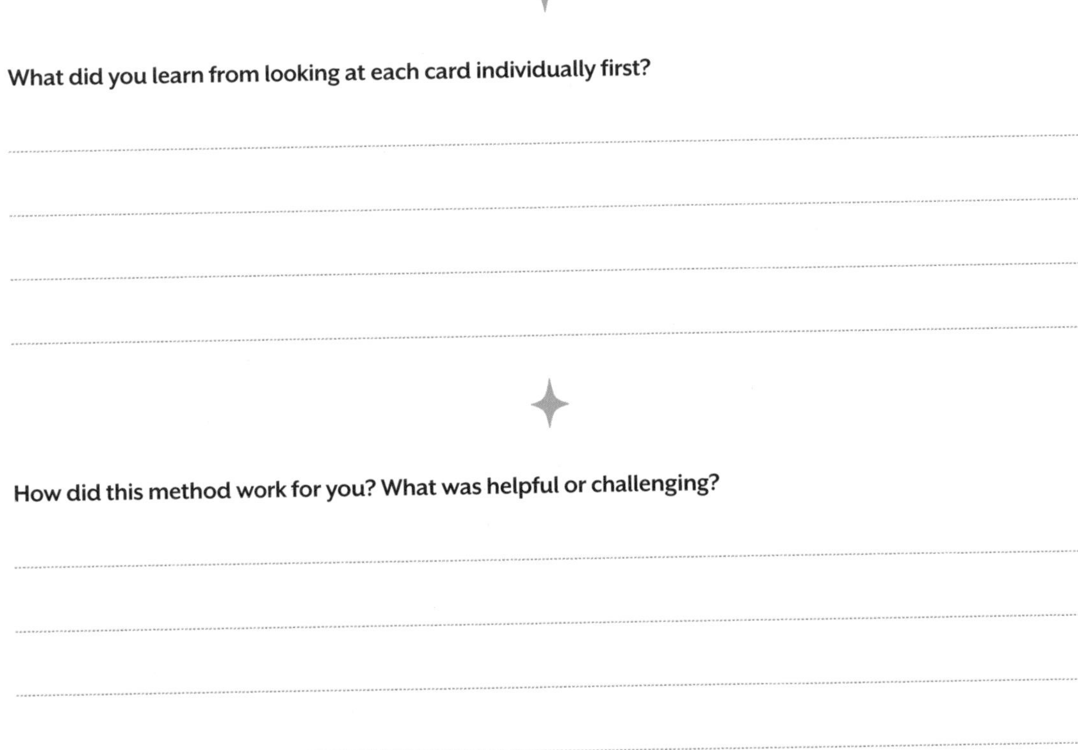
What did you learn from looking at each card individually first?
How did this method work for you? What was helpful or challenging?

Next, start with the cards faceup, so you get to see the interactions and the big picture first. If a certain suit or number is more prevalent than others, it can influence how you read the cards individually, knowing that a specific message is guiding the reading.

What did you learn from seeing the big picture first?

How did this method work for you? What was helpful or challenging?

FIVE-CARD SPREADS

Five-card spreads are a great way to start getting comfortable with new shapes and card placements, as well as all the additional information you get from the extra two cards. There are several different shapes that can be made using only five cards, but here we'll look at two common options that are intuitive to use and easy to customize to suit your deck, questions, and answers.

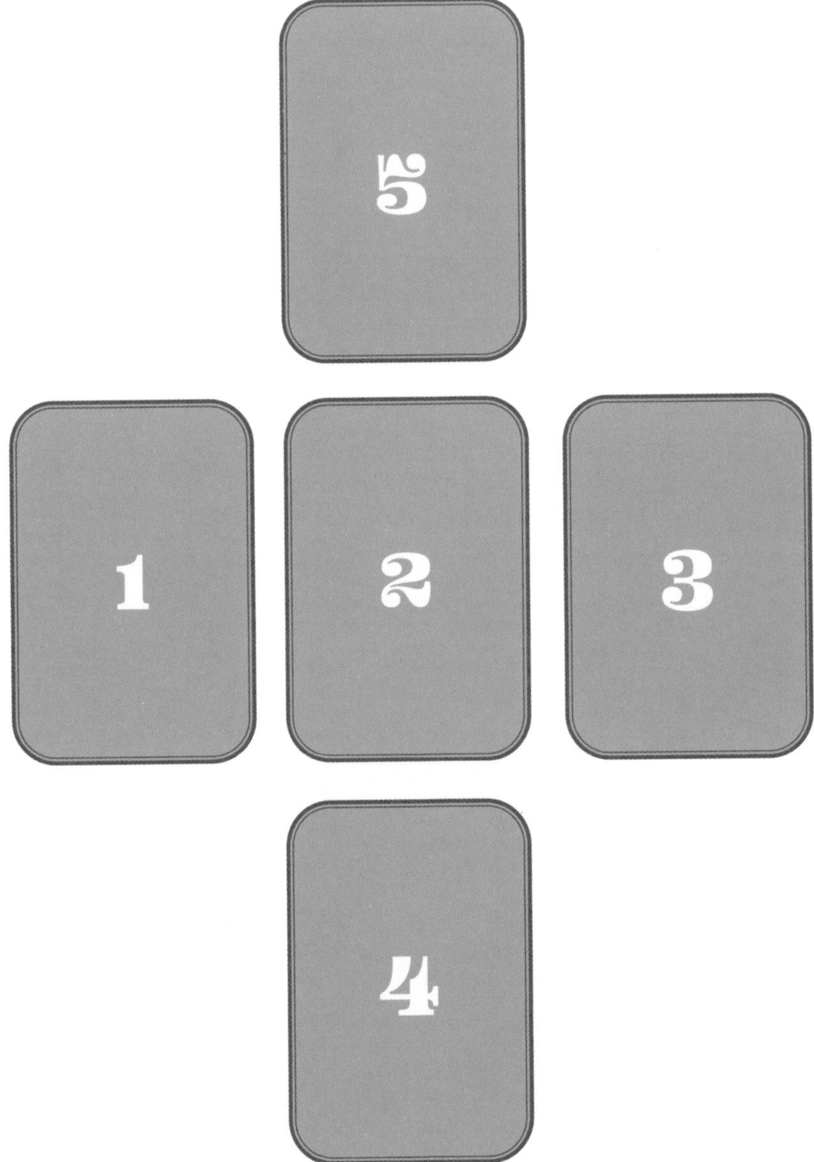

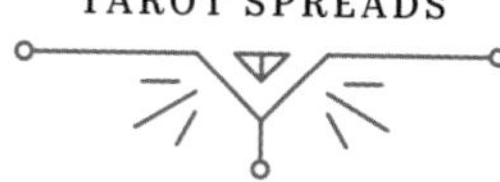

This spread can be an expansion of a three-card spread, with two additional cards offering clarity and more advice. You can expand on any previous spread, using the visual of the positions of cards 4 and 5 as outside of the original three, to indicate that you are likely looking at outside sources of information.

For example, if you are looking at 1-2-3 as

1. Problem
2. Solution
3. Unseen Difficulty

Then 4 and 5 could be read as

4. Subconscious Knowledge
5. Outside Forces

This is another great opportunity to use your intuition to figure out what answers in this shape make the most sense to your understanding of the cards and the question that you are asking.

Fill in your own version below, noting which part of the answer goes with each card. Then try it out, and note your interpretation.

1. ....
2. ....
3. ....
4. ....
5. ....

QUESTION: ....

CARDS

1. ....
2. ....
3. ....
4. ....
5. ....

INTERPRETATION: ....

....

....

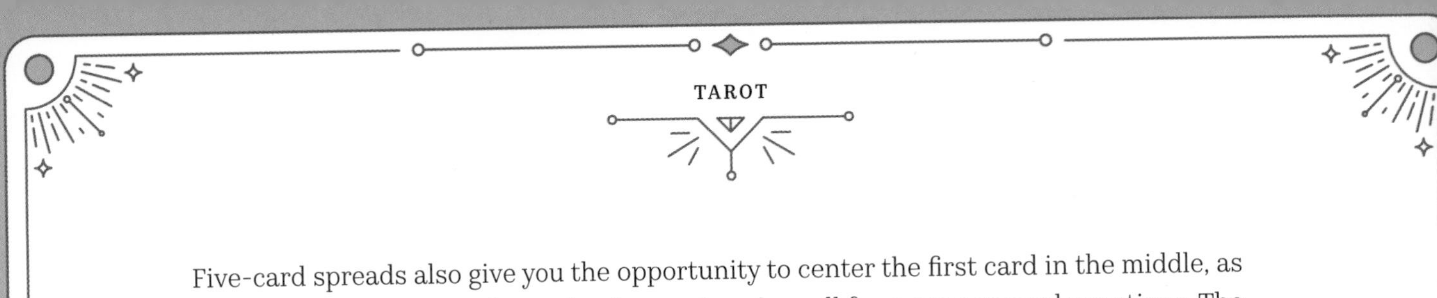

Five-card spreads also give you the opportunity to center the first card in the middle, as an indicator of the self. This style of spread works well for more personal questions. The number 1 is at the heart of the matter, the same way your heart is centered in your body.

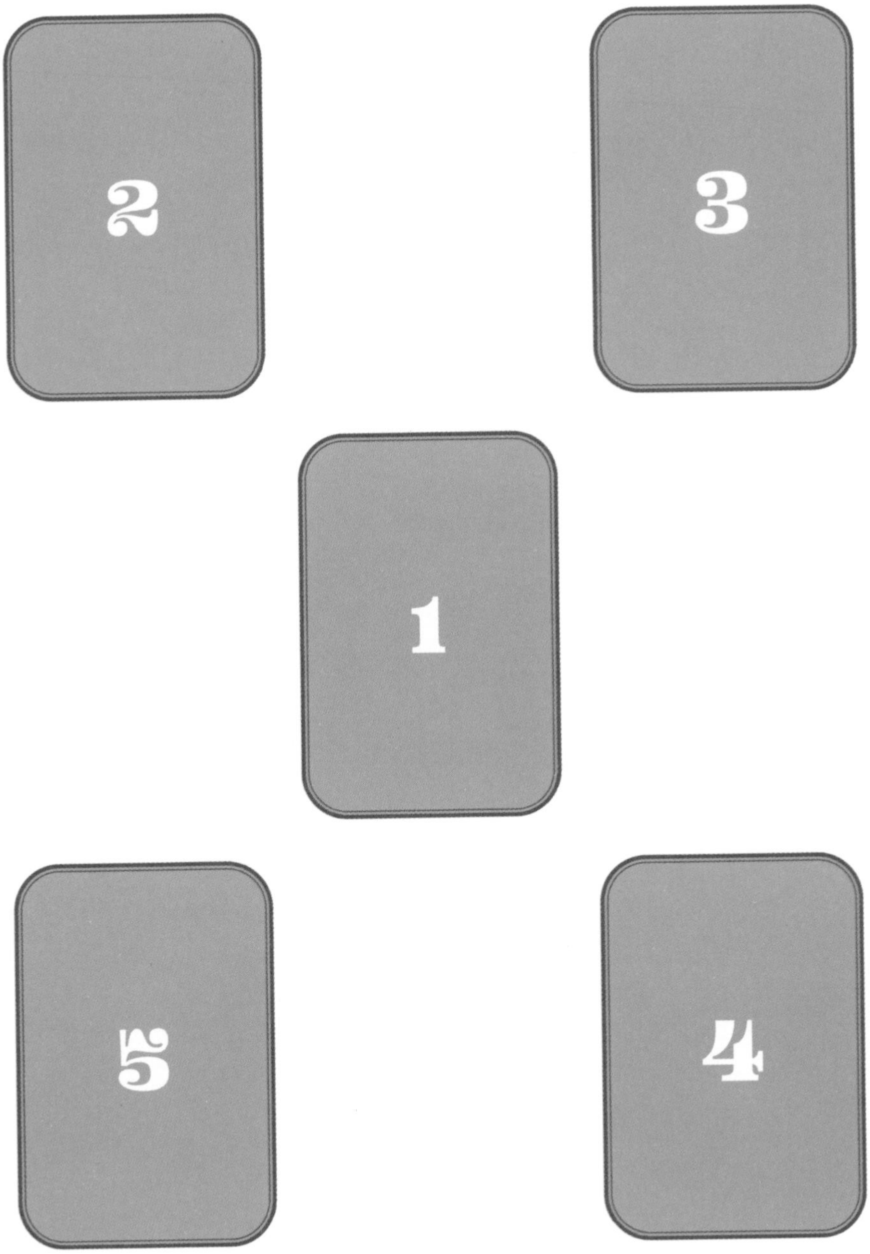

2

3

1

5

4

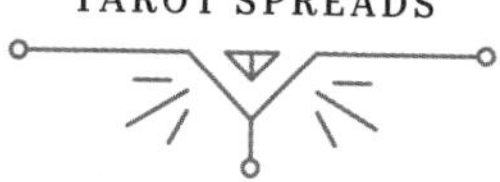

As for the remaining cards, they can appear in any order, and with any meanings that feel appropriate for you. Clockwise can feel like a natural way of dealing out the cards, with the energy of the answers encircling the center, but if your question lends itself to a different order or direction, do not feel held to this configuration.

For cards 2 to 4, look for answers that will support the center of the layout. An example might look like:

2. What you need

3. What you want

4. Next action

5. Decision

Fill in your own version below, noting which part of the answer goes with each card. Then try it out, and note your interpretations.

1. ....

2. ....

3. ....

4. ....

5. ....

QUESTION: ....

CARDS

1. ....

2. ....

3. ....

4. ....

5. ....

INTERPRETATION: ....

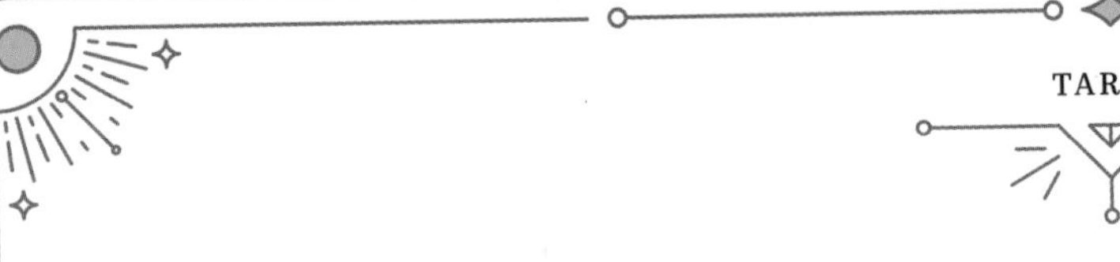

NINE-CARD SPREAD

Once you are comfortable with the meanings of the cards, the way to ask questions, and the basic spreads from earlier in this chapter, moving up to larger spreads with more cards will be a natural progression. In addition to looking at the cards individually, looking at which suits, numbers, or symbols are prominent in the spread can be an important additional step to reading your cards and giving you even more insight that you wouldn't have gotten with a smaller spread.

The same way that a one-card question was turned into a three-card spread, an easy way to transition to a larger spread is to take a three-card spread and expand it to a nine-card spread. The first part of the answer will now be given by cards 1, 2, and 3, with cards 2 and 3 clarifying and adding detail to card 1. The second answer will now be addressed by 4, 5, and 6, and finally the last part of the question will be answered by cards 7, 8, and 9.

Using one of the three-card spreads you tried earlier, or experimenting with a new version, fill in your own answers for a nine-card spread below, noting which part of the answer goes with each set of cards. Then try it out and note your interpretations. The previous page shows one way of arranging this spread. If you find that working top-down or horizontally is more intuitive to your reading, trust your gut and go for it.

1. ______

4. ______

7. ______

QUESTION: ______

CARDS

1. ______
2. ______
3. ______
4. ______
5. ______
6. ______
7. ______
8. ______
9. ______

INTERPRETATION: ______

PYRAMID SPREAD

Pyramid spreads are great for focusing on questions that build on each other. Below is a basic ten-card pyramid, but if more rows are called for, it can easily be increased to fifteen or even twenty-one cards. If fewer rows are needed, remove the bottom row for a useful six-card spread. These spreads tend to work best from bottom-to-top, with the more concrete parts of the answer at the base, moving up to the more abstract or theoretical. They can be most easily read with all the cards of each row answering the same question.

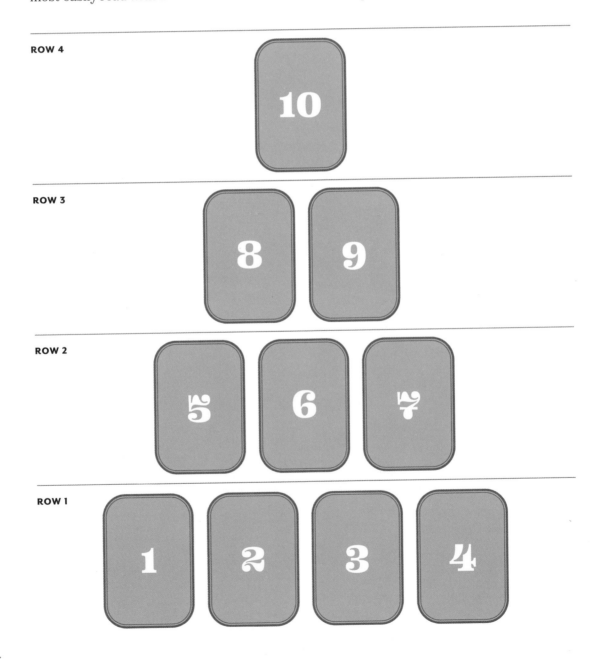

ROW 4 10

ROW 3 8 9

ROW 2 5 6 7

ROW 1 1 2 3 4

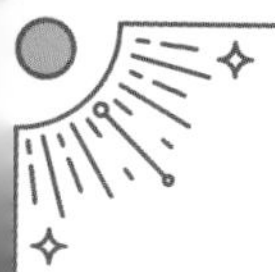

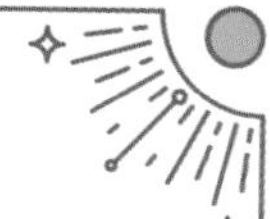

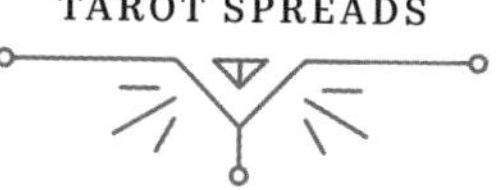

Below are two ways to read a ten-card pyramid spread, but there are many possibilities:

ROW 1: Your present inner truth

ROW 2: Possible near future

ROW 3: Hopes and fears

ROW 4: Outcome

OR

ROW 1: Root cause of the situation

ROW 2: What steps need to be taken to move forward

ROW 3: Things to consider when making a decision

ROW 4: Final result

Choose one of these methods, and try out the spread for yourself.

ROW 1: ....

ROW 2: ....

ROW 3: ....

ROW 4: ....

QUESTION: ....

CARDS

1. ....
2. ....
3. ....
4. ....
5. ....
6. ....
7. ....
8. ....
9. ....
10. ....

INTERPRETATION: ....

CELTIC CROSS

The Celtic Cross is one of the most recognizable spreads in tarot. This spread can give you a huge amount of information and is great to do as a check-in at regular intervals of time, or after major shifts in your life. As with any spread, there are variations on what each card means. The key is to get an understanding of the spread itself and focus on what each placement indicates for you. This is only one example. If you find different card orders or answers to be more intuitive for you, do what feels best for you.

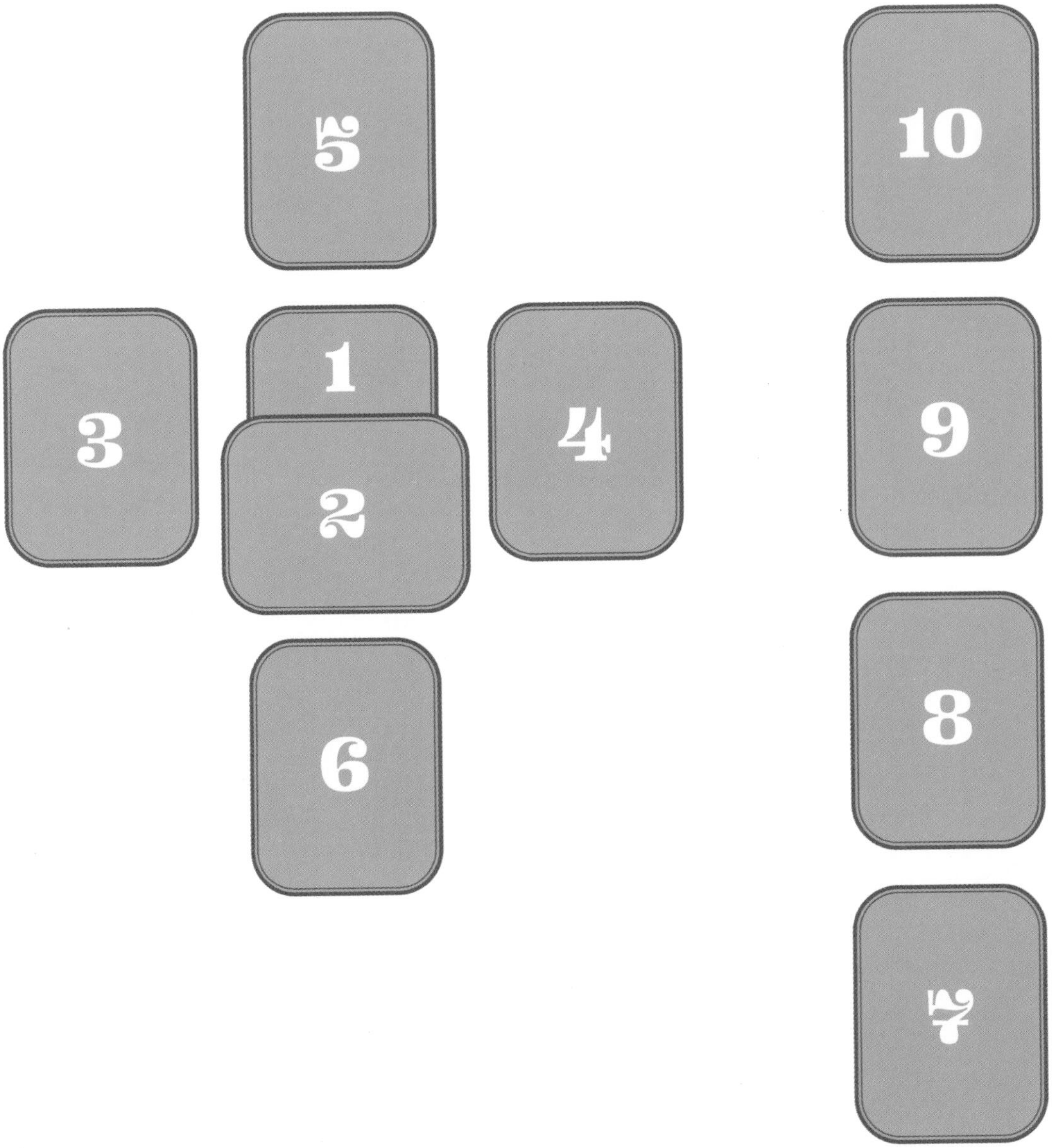

5

10

3 1 2 4

9

8

6

7

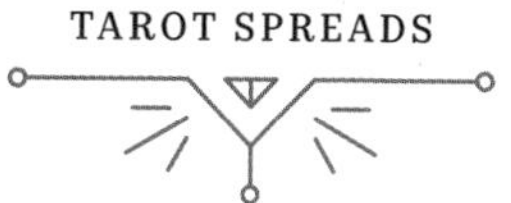

1. **THE PRESENT**–This card represents you at this moment in time.
2. **THE CHALLENGE**–This card will tell you what is having the greatest impact on the question asked. This is what can be corrected by following the path and advice of the other cards in the reading.
3. **THE PAST**–This card represents the parts of the past that are still influencing the issue.
4. **THE FUTURE**–This card represents the likely next step in your process. It is the immediate future, what you'll be able to move toward.
5. **YOUR GOAL**–This card will show you the best possible solution to the problem at hand.
6. **YOUR SUBCONSCIOUS**–This card will show you a truth that you might not have been able to face before now that is influencing what is happening.
7. **INNER TRUTH**–This card is advice that you know: your gut instinct on what you should do.
8. **OUTSIDE ADVICE/INFLUENCES**–This card will show you additional guidance from an outside perspective and show you what outside of yourself is affecting the situation.
9. **HOPES AND FEARS**–While only one card, our hopes and fears are often two sides of the same coin. Use this card to determine what hasn't been solidified or is holding you back.
10. **THE OUTCOME**–This is the resolution that the path you've read will lead you to. Note that this is only one possible outcome: the future can always be changed.

Try out the Celtic Cross for yourself.

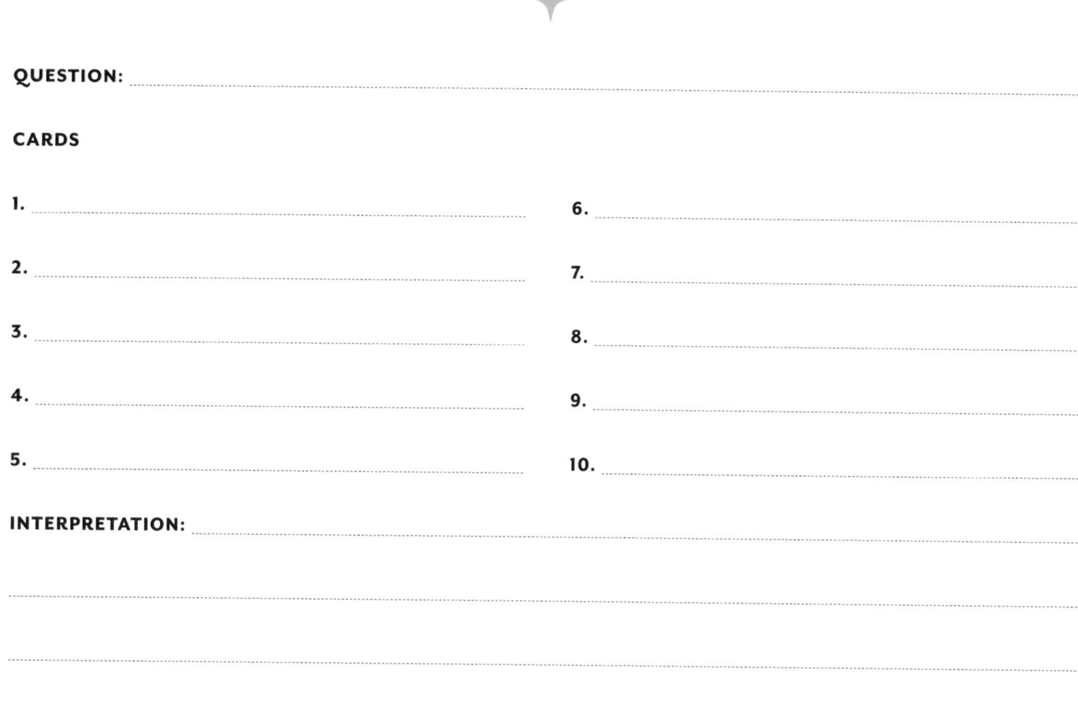

QUESTION: ....

CARDS

1.	**6.** ....
2.	**7.** ....
3.	**8.** ....
4.	**9.** ....
5.	**10.** ....

INTERPRETATION: ....

....

....

....

CONSIDER THE SUITS

As you read larger spreads, you may start to notice a certain suit makes up the majority of the spread. We must always pay attention to this majority, as it can show us where we should be focusing our attention. Sometimes, the focus may not seem to align with the question we've asked, but even that can give us an insight we may not have seen otherwise. For example, if we are asking questions about a romantic relationship, and pull a majority of Swords, we should bring our awareness to the fact that we are likely overthinking matters of the heart.

Choose one of the larger spreads and ask a question. Shuffle and meditate on the question and each answer as you pull each card and place it in the spread.

WHICH SPREAD DID YOU READ? ....

QUESTION: ....

INTERPRETATION: ....

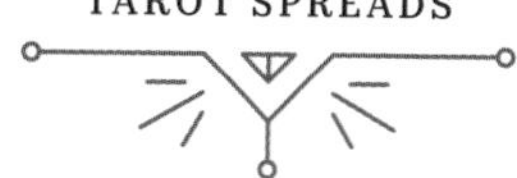

CIRCLE THE CARDS THAT HAVE THE MAJORITY IN THE SPREAD.

MAJOR ARCANA	PENTACLES	CUPS	WANDS	SWORDS

HOW DOES THIS SUIT'S PROMINENCE AFFECT THE OVERALL READING OF THE CARDS?

BUILD YOUR OWN LARGE SPREAD

Once you've practiced a few spreads, create a spread that speaks to you individually.

As you've seen through the work in this chapter, there are many answers that repeatedly occur in spreads. Below is a list of some of the most common, and room for your own additions.

SELF	OBSTACLES	OUTSIDE FORCES
PAST	SOLUTIONS	STRENGTHS
PRESENT	OPTIONS	WEAKNESSES
FUTURE	HOPES	PROBLEMS
INNER TRUTH	FEARS	ACTIONS
HIDDEN POTENTIAL	DECISIONS	POSSIBLE OUTCOME
WANTS	NEEDS	CHANGES

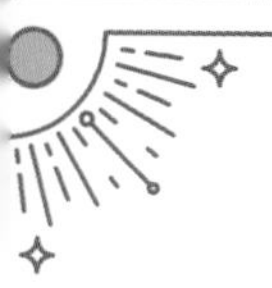
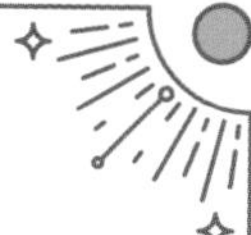

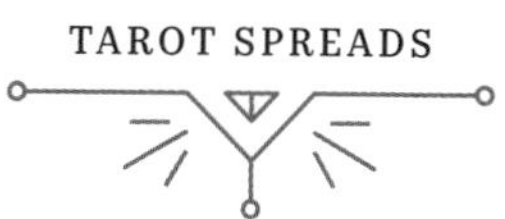

Circle the answers that you'd like to see in your spread. How many cards does each part of your spread require? Can they each be answered by one card, or do any of them require additional influence cards? Do any of the answers need multiple possibilities?

HOW MANY ANSWERS DID YOU CIRCLE TO USE IN YOUR SPREAD? ....

HOW MANY CARDS WILL YOU BE PULLING FOR YOUR SPREAD? ....

Next, consider the shape of your spread. If there was a shape in the chapter that spoke to you, see if you can use that as a basis to build from. If you feel drawn to another shape, go with it. The possibilities are endless, and the more connected you feel to each part of the spread, the more effective it will be.

Gather the number of cards you'll need and try out different shapes to see what feels right. You can use rectangles, circles, pyramids, crescents, trees, spirals, or anything else that comes to mind. Take your time and try different placements of the cards until you come up with a layout that speaks to you.

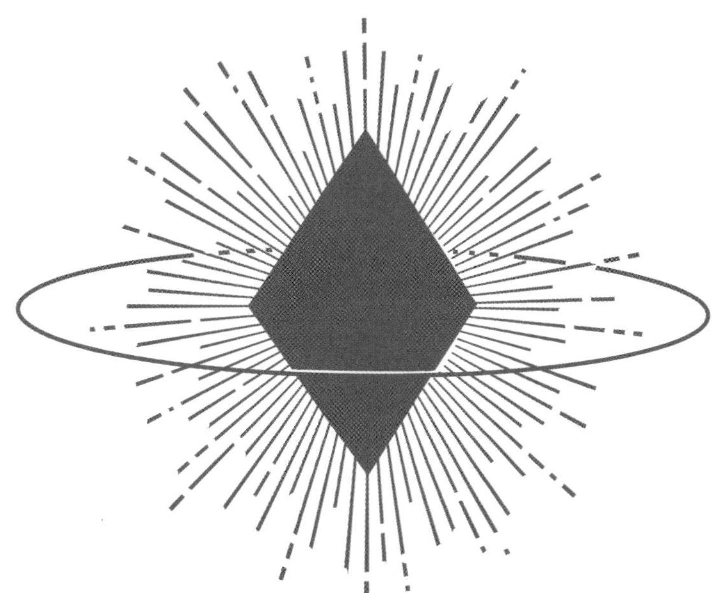

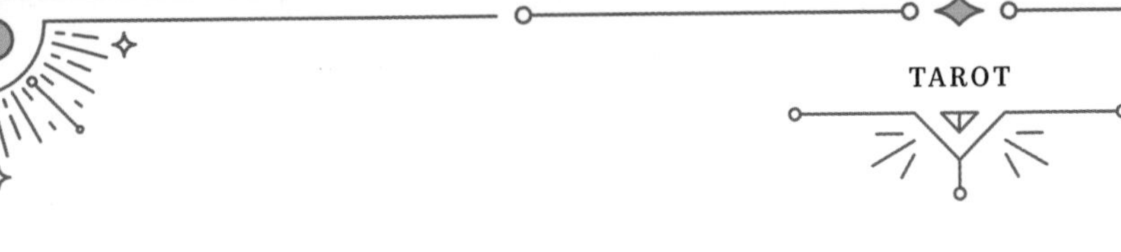

Use the space on this page to sketch out the layout of the spread that you've settled on. Once you're happy with the shape, figure out the placement of each answer and the order they should be pulled in.

You can see from this chapter that some spreads start in the center and build around a first card, while others are read bottom to top or left to right. Think about what makes you feel most connected to the cards. When you've sketched out the shape, mark each card with the number and the answer that it represents. Use this as your guide for the next page where you'll do a reading of your spread, and see how well it works for you.

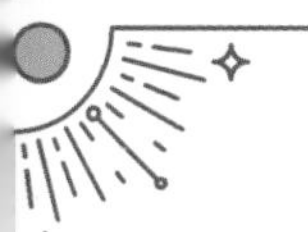

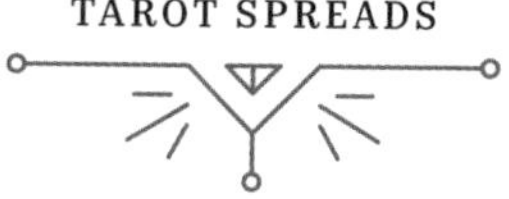

Use your spread to ask a question and read for yourself.

QUESTION

INTERPRETATION

WHAT TYPES OF QUESTIONS IS THIS SPREAD BEST SUITED FOR?

WHAT WORKED BEST?

SHOULD ANY CHANGES BE MADE TO MAKE THIS SPREAD MORE EFFECTIVE?

The spread possibilities are endless, which can be both empowering and overwhelming. As you become more comfortable using your cards and practicing different spreads, your favorites will emerge and become second nature to you. You can revisit the exercises in this chapter as often as you need to and continue exploring different ways to arrange your cards so that they are most meaningful to you. Tarot reading is a practice, and you'll see how your style and understanding continues to evolve over time.

NOTES